The Ultimate CPA Practice in the New Economy

---

10 Secrets to Attract More Clients,
Boost Profits and Live Your Ideal Lifestyle

Salim Omar, CPA

Disclaimer: This publication is designed to provide accurate and authoritative information in regard to the subject matter covered. It is sold with the understanding that the publisher is not engaged in rendering legal, accounting or other professional services. If legal advice or other expert assistance is required, the services of a professional person should be sought.

ISBN-13: 978-0615564265

Published by:

Saza Publishing House
49 Cliffwood Avenue, Suite 200
Cliffwood, NJ 07721

Praise For The Book

"Most accountants stink at marketing--either because they're too shy, too busy or too ignorant about the hundreds of things they can do to position themselves as experts, find leads and close the deal. Salim Omar clearly gets it.

By using a variety of smart marketing strategies, tactics and tools, he grew his struggling practice into a thriving eight-person accounting firm.

Now, Omar pulls back the curtain to reveal the many things he did to toot his own horn and end up on the cover of Accounting Today magazine. His 12-month "Client Touch Plan," which you can use as a helpful cheat sheet, is worth more than the price of this book."

Joan Stewart
PublicityHound.com

"In this handy book, you've got a comprehensive guide to the strategies and tactics you need to market an accounting practice."

Michael McLaughlin
Principal, MindShare Consulting LLC
Publisher, Management Consulting News

"This is the "go to" manual for the practitioner looking for one source for all the proven practices of successful CPA firms. Omar has captured in one place the broad range of competencies and methodologies that will lead to success. This book is a roadmap and, if followed, will enable CPAs to implement best practices in the most important areas of CPA firm business operations. This book is a treasure trove of the tools to bring your practice to the next level. He is right on here, the wisdom on these pages works and we have seen it first-hand."

Ed Guttenplan, CPA, MBA
Managing Shareholder, Wilkin & Guttenplan, PC

"In The Ultimate CPA Practice in the New Economy, Salim Omar presents one of the most thorough and logical guides to building and developing a successful professional services practice I have seen.

Omar takes the practitioner step by step through the process of identifying who they are, what they bring to the table for their potential clients, and most importantly, how to free themselves from the minutia of their practice in order to be able to build their practice.

If you want to build your practice while freeing yourself from the tyranny of 100-hour work weeks, get a copy of The Ultimate CPA Practice in the New Economy and implement Omar's sage advice—you'll find that not only will you be growing your practice, but you'll also be reclaiming control of your life."

Paul McCord, Author: Creating a Million Dollar a Year Sales Income President, McCord Training

"This is a great resource for any CPA who wants to increase their effectiveness AND enhance their lives WHILE growing their CPA practice. What I especially like is that Salim has obviously done it! This book not only outlines the "what to do" but more importantly "HOW to do it.""

Peter Schwartz
Vistage Chair

"Marketing accounting services today is less about expertise and skills sets and much more about the experience that the client has with their accounting firm. Salim Omar's book is a great manual for any firm wishing to leverage the power of creating a unique client experience and maximizing the client's level of engagement that consistently delivers profitable business in today's market"

Seán Weafer
Author: ClientEQ – How to Find, Close and Keep High Net Worth

Dedicated to my mother,
who taught me to never quit
and to stay the course,
even when the going was tough.

About the Author

SALIM OMAR is an accountant with a passion for helping other small business owners and CPAs succeed.

In addition to helping his clients build more profitable businesses, he is committed to teaching other CPAs how to attract more clients and increase their income, while enjoying their lives more.

As a former chief financial officer, Salim knows what clients seek from a CPA. In fifteen years running his own successful CPA practice in New Jersey, he has discovered what works – and what doesn't – in building a profitable CPA practice.

He is a highly sought-after speaker and author of the popular book *Straight Talk About Small Business Success In New Jersey*. His articles have been published nationwide in prestigious industry publications such as *Accounting Today, The CPA Journal,* and *Financial Advisor.*

Salim has also created several programs to help CPAs grow their practices, including the *Genius CPA Marketing System* and the *CPA Referral Genius System*.

His education includes a unique blend of three financially-based accreditations: a master's degree in accounting, certified public accountant, and registered investment advisor.

He has also extensively studied business success and marketing, learning directly from top business and marketing experts such as Michael Gerber, Jay Abraham, Dan Kennedy, Mark Victor Hansen, and Gary Halbert.

Salim's philosophy is that by following the right approach, CPAs and entrepreneurs can enjoy their businesses – and lives – more fully, even in difficult economic times.

Table of Contents

Introduction: Discovering The Ultimate CPA Practice xiii
   The Keys to Dramatic Change xiv
   How The Dream Of Starting My Own Practice Went Awry xv
   Looking Out Of The Box for A Solution xvi
   Creating A Thriving Practice and Having A Life....................xvii
   Why Any CPA Can Achieve This xviii
   The 10 Secrets Of The Ultimate CPA Practice xix
   Why Now Is The Time for Change xx

Chapter 1. Preparing for Success:
Setting Up Your Practice for Higher Profits While Working Less.........*1*
   The Genius CPA Mindset – Seven Key Principles Of Success.........2

Chapter 2. Positioning and Planning:
Standing Out From The Competition to Become First Choice In
Your Market *41*
   Defining Your Market — The "Who" 43
   Establishing A Clear Message — The "Why" 50
   Choosing The Right Media — The "How" 55

Chapter 3. Personal Branding:
Establishing Yourself As An Expert So That Prospects and Clients
Start Contacting You *61*
   Identifying Your Specific Field Of Expertise 63
   Choosing The Best Tools to Promote Your Expertise 65
   Leveraging Everything for Maximum Benefit 78

Chapter 4. Promotion and Advertising:
Getting Your Practice's Message Across to Your Target Market *83*

Two-Step Marketing 86
Genius Marketing Tools 87
Genius Marketing Techniques 94

Chapter 5. Powerful Online Presence:
Using The Internet Effectively to Reach More People and Build Your Brand *105*

Creating Your Online Home 106
7 Strategies for Driving Traffic to Your Website 113
Turning Visitors Into Clients 121
Social Media Strategies 122
Tracking and Analytics 125

Chapter 6. Profitable Client Relationships:
Growing Your Profits The Easy Way By Getting Closer to Existing Clients *131*

Knowing How Much Each Client Is Worth 133
Seven Ways to Build Relationships With Clients
So They Spend More 135
Your Client Touch Plan 152

Chapter 7. Pricing and Packaging:
Secrets to Ensuring Your Clients and Prospects Will Happily Pay More for Your Services *157*

Why Hourly Rates Are Detrimental for You and Your Clients ... 160
How to Price Your Services Based On Value 162
Packaging Your Services for Higher Profit 171
Promoting and Cross-Selling A Wider Range Of Your Services ... 175

Chapter 8. Partnership With Clients:
How Your Clients Will Help You Build Your Practice *179*

How to Collect and Use Powerful Testimonials............................ 180
How to Generate A Steady Stream Of Referrals 188
It's Not Only Clients Who Give Referrals 197

Chapter 9. People and Profits:
Hiring and Motivating Great Employees Who Contribute More to Profits and Success... *203*

Hiring The Best People 204
Retaining and Motivating The Best Performers 207
Ensuring Staff Contribute Fully to Success 211

Chapter 10. Persuasive Selling Skills:
Enhancing Your Ability to Get Clients to Say "Yes" More Often *217*

Closing Sales With New Prospects 218
Following Up On Unconverted Leads... 224
Contacting Previous Clients 226

Moving to The Next Level **231**
Genius CPA Marketing System 232
CPA Referral Genius System 233
Superstar CPA Program.. 234
Genius CPA Private Coaching 236

Index... 241
Reader-Only Special Bonus ($328 Value)....................................... 247

Acknowledgments

There are three groups of people without whom this book would never have been more than a dream.

First, I want to acknowledge those mentors, teachers and advisers who showed me the correct path when I had so clearly taken the wrong one before. I mention some of them at various stages in this book, but there are also others whose guidance helped me turn my practice around and create the lifestyle I now enjoy. To all of them I offer my thanks for their inspiration and leadership.

Secondly, I want to say a special word to those CPAs who have worked with me in recent years to learn the strategies that have helped me succeed. Working with you has helped me discover faster and more effective routes to success. You have taught me much, and your friendship and support motivates and inspires me. Again I have mentioned a handful in this book. To those of you who contributed to this book, as well as the rest who have helped me in countless other ways, I offer my heartfelt gratitude.

Finally, a word of thanks to my colleagues and clients in my CPA practice. My clients are my lifeblood and the reason I succeed in business. Helping you get better results is what inspires me to push forward to new levels of success. None of that would be possible without my excellent, dedicated team who help me achieve so much more than I could alone. I sincerely appreciate everything that you do.

To all of you, my thanks and admiration. This book is my tribute to you.

Salim

INTRODUCTION:
Discovering the Ultimate CPA Practice

IT FRUSTRATES ME to see so many CPAs working too hard, earning too little, and taking their worries home from the office.

It bothers me because I know it doesn't have to be like that.

We study a great deal to achieve our qualifications and work hard to help our clients, so we should all be able to enjoy the satisfaction and rewards that come from providing a valuable service.

The problem is that throughout these years we spend learning and developing our technical knowledge, very little – if any – time is devoted to teaching the essential business skills that help us benefit from what we do.

We don't learn the strategies that help us to promote our expertise, earn what we are worth and build the kind of practice or career we would like. That means too many CPAs don't enjoy the financial rewards and personal satisfaction that they really should.

I've seen many of the most stressful and unsatisfying aspects of a CPA career.

I've had a highly paid job as a CFO, which I hated because of long hours and too much office politics.

I also spent way too much time struggling to run a small practice where I couldn't sleep at night worrying whether I'd earn enough that month to pay my mortgage and feed my family. It really was that precarious.

Yet now, I typically work three or four days a week and have no problem attracting high-paying clients to my practice. I'm recognized as a go-to expert in my area. In fact, my success story was recently noticed by *Accounting Today* and I was featured on the cover of the magazine.

My life changed dramatically by following these principles – and the same is possible for you.

THE KEYS TO DRAMATIC CHANGE

Truth be told, there is nothing special about me. I simply found myself in a situation where – deep in debt – I had to change what I was doing in order to get different results.

I've probably made every mistake possible and I certainly experienced a few struggles along the way. However, I was able to completely turn things around.

These days, one of my driving passions is helping other CPAs engineer the same turnaround in their practices and in their lives.

I like to think of those who prosper in the current market conditions as "Genius CPAs."

That's not because you have to be any smarter than anyone else to succeed. It's because when you apply the right strategies, you will stand apart from the vast majority of your competition and achieve strikingly better results.

You will discover that it really is possible to work less and earn more – if you follow the right steps.

In this book, I have shared the mindset, strategies, and tools that have helped me to create a highly profitable practice and, just as important, to start living the lifestyle I had previously only dreamed about.

I'll show you exactly how you can join the ranks of the Genius CPAs – and have the Ultimate CPA Practice – regardless of where you are currently with your practice or career.

However, more on that later. Let me start by explaining a little of how I got to where I am today.

HOW THE DREAM OF STARTING MY OWN PRACTICE WENT AWRY

It was June 1996. I was sitting in a nice plush corner office overlooking Central Park, perhaps one of the most glamorous pieces of real estate in NYC. The office was a penthouse and the tenant beneath us was Playboy Enterprises, Inc.

As CFO of a New York City-based corporation, I was a key member of the executive committee and had a team of accountants working for me. I was making a very comfortable living.

But truthfully, I was miserable. I hated the stress, the long commute, the hours, and the corporate politics.

So the day I left that career to set up my own CPA practice was one of the most exciting and liberating days of my life.

I was confident – perhaps too confident. As my dad had been in the retail business, I was around business a lot growing up and we'd discuss it pretty much every night over dinner. I thought I knew a lot about what was needed to succeed.

The truth is that I didn't know enough about running a business, and from the beginning I struggled.

Fast forward five years to 2001. I was sitting in my more modest office in New Jersey. I was still highly stressed, but this time I didn't have the consolation of a comfortable income. The reality was quite the opposite.

I had invested in a widely-promoted system that was designed to generate regular leads for my practice. In addition to the huge up-front cost, it was costing me around $75,000 a year in operating expenses.

The problem was that it didn't work as well as I wanted it to. While it brought in some clients, they were not high-quality clients and I was ultimately losing a lot of money.

My practice was becoming a drain on my savings. I was logging 70 to 80 hour weeks and was a stranger in my own home. Moreover, I was more than $100,000 in debt and running out of money.

You can imagine the stress I was feeling and the worry that it was causing my family.

My first five years or so in practice could hardly have been more challenging. I came pretty close to quitting the practice and trying to find another job.

This was not the way I had dreamed it would be when I decided to escape the anxieties of my previous life. But that seemed nothing compared to the worries of possibly losing my home and letting my family down.

LOOKING OUT OF THE BOX FOR A SOLUTION

I knew I had to do something. And it had to be something dramatic. So I made a complete change. I turned my back on the marketing approaches that the so-called "gurus" were selling to CPAs.

Instead of being boxed in by the failed old CPA solutions, I looked *out* of the box.

I went to "school," read every book and course on marketing that I could find and I attended every seminar that I possibly could. I was learning from the thought leaders in the world.

I invested in learning from people like Michael Gerber – author of *The E-Myth* series – who made me realize that I was approaching the whole idea of running a business the wrong way.

I studied and worked with two of the most respected (and most copied) marketing strategists of our time – Jay Abraham and Dan Kennedy. They opened my eyes to the strategies and tactics that truly lead to marketing success.

And I devoured everything from copywriting geniuses such as John Carlton and the late Gary Halbert. They taught me what I needed to do to stand out from the competition.

However, with all of that knowledge at my fingertips, there is one factor that had a bigger impact than any other in my turnaround:

I took action and I implemented what I learned in my practice.

CREATING A THRIVING PRACTICE AND HAVING A LIFE

I used my practice as a real-time laboratory to find out what worked and what didn't. I had some great successes and some absolute bombs.

I was spending a lot of money on improving my business-building skills, but I was being fed from a good source and it was worth every penny.

And it worked (thank goodness!).

- Instead of chasing after prospects, they were calling me.

- Within eight months, I signed up 18 new business clients and a flood of personal tax clients.

- For the last five years, I've signed about two or three new business clients every month.

- Consistent cash flow covers my expenses and puts growing profits in my pocket every month.

Best of all, I have a thriving practice and my life back.

I have realized that I don't need to involve myself in every day-to-day technical detail of the practice and of my clients. Instead, I trust my dedicated and competent employees to do their jobs. It's better for them too as they are now happy coming to work every day.

In addition, I focus my time and energy on the tasks appropriate to being the owner of the practice. That has freed up my time so that I work only four seven-hour days each week during tax season and three days a week the rest of the year. And I enjoy at least five weeks of vacation every year.

As a matter of fact, as I write this book, I am in the process of planning my fifth vacation for the year (with some philanthropic purpose as well). It will most likely be a trip to Kenya (the country where I was born and spent the first twenty years of my life) with a two-day stop in Europe.

The truth is the Genius CPA not only makes more profits in their practice, they also enjoy a better life.

WHY ANY CPA CAN ACHIEVE THIS

While I am naturally very happy that my own practice and life have improved so much as a result of what I learned, the most exciting part for me is that I have been able to help other CPAs make the same huge transformation in their lives.

I am thrilled that others have been able to follow the Genius CPA approach and enjoy the same results.

- They are growing their revenue while others are barely keeping their heads above water.

- Their clients are fanatically loyal and willing to pay premium fees in return for superior service.

- They can cut their marketing costs because their clients regularly send them high quality referrals.

- They have their pick of the best talent in their market (and their staff stays loyal even if they are offered more money elsewhere).

- Their practices effortlessly win client after client.

These principles apply equally to those who are partners or professionals working in a larger practice. You may be tempted to skip over some of these points if you feel they are outside of your control and not part of your responsibility.

The reality is that the path to success these days – as we move into a new economy – is always being able to think of yourself as an owner even when you are not.

If you want to build the best possible career now, you need to be able to think of yourself as CEO of "You Inc." even when you are employed in a larger firm.

The fact of the matter is that the more you can bring these skills and knowledge to the practice, the more value you are delivering to your employer and the more chance you have of pushing your career forward to higher levels and increased earnings.

THE 10 SECRETS OF THE ULTIMATE CPA PRACTICE

From my own experience – and from working directly with so many other Genius CPAs – I have discovered several keys to the mindset and strategies for creating the kind of practice that delivers results.

In this book, I'm going to share 10 Secrets of the Ultimate CPA Practice with you. These include how to:

- Prepare your practice for success by developing the "owner mindset" and creating effective working systems.

- Position your practice as the first choice in a clearly defined, profitable market.

- Create a strong Personal Brand that establishes you as a recognized expert so that prospective clients start contacting you.

- Promote your practice using proven and effective genius marketing tools and techniques.

- Build a Powerful Online Presence that attracts large numbers of highly-targeted prospects and clients.

- Develop effective strategies and systems to develop Profitable Relationships with the right clients.

- Price and Package your services so that you charge the right fees and increase your involvement with your clients.

- Partner with your clients by having them help you grow through referrals and testimonials.

- Hire and motivate the right People so that they contribute more to the success and Profits of your practice.

- Develop strong Persuasive Selling Skills so that you find it easier to sign up new clients and develop more profitable relationships.

WHY NOW IS THE TIME FOR CHANGE

The fact is that it's getting tougher than ever to grow a profitable CPA practice.

Many of our clients and prospects are looking for ways to cut back on costs. This, added to the growth of accounting software, makes some people place less value on CPA services. If we don't know how to ensure our clients value our services, we face a downward spiral of fees.

The other concern is that traditional marketing approaches like old-style networking are no longer as effective – so we need to find new ways to reach out to prospective new clients. The growing importance of new channels, such as online marketing and social media, means firms which stick to the old approaches are at a huge disadvantage.

If your practice is currently going according to plan and you are enjoying a great lifestyle, then I'm not in the business of telling you that my way is better.

However, if you are not achieving the kind of profits you need – or you feel you are simply working too many hours for the reward you are getting – you're likely to find that making a change pays huge dividends.

If you are ready to try a proven approach to practice growth and make some changes in how you work, you could reach new levels of success.

There probably has never been a more important time to learn the secrets of the Ultimate CPA Practice.

There are steps you can take right now to switch over to the Genius CPA approach. I'll explain each of them as you work through the 10 Secrets in this book.

- I'll give you a series of Action Steps you can take to start seeing results right away.

- Also, I will share Genius CPA Insights to highlight important changes you may need to make in the way you think and work.

- Plus, at the end of each chapter, I'll share Top Mistakes to Avoid to help you become a Genius CPA faster.

These will work for you whether you are:

- Just starting out in your practice.

- An established practitioner looking to reach new heights of success.

- Working as a partner or professional in a larger firm.

They will also work regardless of the services you provide, such as write up, tax planning, tax preparation, IRS tax resolution, assurance, attest and audit services, financial and estate planning, or specialty services such as business valuation, forensic accounting, management consulting, or CFO-type services.

The Genius CPA approach has positively impacted my life and that of many other CPAs not only throughout the United States, but also across the world in countries including Australia, Britain, Canada, Puerto Rico, Ireland, and New Zealand.

Throughout this book, several CPAs share how they and their practices have benefited by applying my teachings.

If you are ready to make some changes and take action, what you learn in this book could transform your practice and your life forever.

Salim Omar, CPA

PREPARING FOR SUCCESS:

Setting Up Your Practice for Higher Profits While Working Less

----

"No one ever attains very eminent success by simply doing what is required of him; it is the amount and excellence of what is over and above the required that determines the greatness of ultimate distinction."

CHARLES KENDALL ADAMS
HISTORIAN, 1835 - 1902

THERE IS ONE SECTION of the bookstore that has made a big difference in my life.

You see, I have been a student of "self-help" (aka "motivational stuff") for the past 25 years or so.

The section of the bookstore that carried those titles was my favorite and I would automatically gravitate towards it the moment I entered the store.

As I reflect back, I'm so pleased I discovered this resource – especially during my start-up years – because it fed me with the inspiration, encouragement and support that I so very much needed when things weren't going as well as I had anticipated.

I learned from studying these materials that having the "right mindset" is the single most significant determining factor of success. When we change our mindset, we automatically change our perspective, the way we interpret things, the decisions we make, the actions we take, and the results we get.

As a matter of fact, if you take a look at powerful, successful people the world over, you might be surprised to find that they generally don't have extraordinarily high IQs. Translated to a small-business level, successful practitioners don't have to be the smartest cookie in the jar. Sure, it helps, but it's not a prerequisite.

Many successful business owners and entrepreneurs delight in sharing the fact that they are just ordinary, average people – certainly not superstars worthy of membership at Mensa.

So if these seemingly normal people can achieve such success, how do they do it?

What qualities and characteristics do they exhibit that make them different from the rest of the population? In my opinion, it is that they have the *right mindset*.

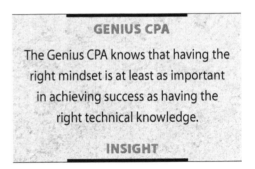

GENIUS CPA

The Genius CPA knows that having the right mindset is at least as important in achieving success as having the right technical knowledge.

INSIGHT

THE GENIUS CPA MINDSET – SEVEN KEY PRINCIPLES OF SUCCESS

When I talk to CPAs about the biggest challenges they face in their practices, what I typically hear about the most is attracting more clients, becoming more profitable, and working fewer hours.

Naturally these are vital in the process of building a more profitable, lifestyle-driven practice.

Yet the problem with putting the focus on attracting more clients is that it can end up simply creating more problems if it is not matched by having the right mindset.

In short, if you want to get Genius CPA results, you need to have a Genius CPA mindset.

As I've said, that's not about having a high IQ. Believe me, if it were, I would be disqualified on that count! It's about following a handful of key principles in the way you approach your work and your practice.

In this chapter, I'm going to focus on seven key success mindset principles you need to put in place as the basis for growing your Genius CPA practice.

These are:

1. Being open to change.

2. Establishing a clear "strategic objective."

3. Working "on" your practice instead of "in" it.

4. Differentiating yourself from the competition.

5. Streamlining your practice by creating effective systems.

6. Making the best use of your time by setting priorities.

7. Becoming extraordinary and creating a world class practice.

We'll now look at each of these principles in detail.

1. BEING OPEN TO CHANGE

I don't know about you, but I love watching movies; and, if at all possible, rather than watching them on TV, I head to a nearby theater to enjoy the gigantic screen and full surround-sound effect (not to mention the popcorn).

One that has stuck in my mind is *A Few Good Men* starring Tom Cruise and Jack Nicholson. I loved this movie – especially the intense court scene towards the end with the classic line from Jack Nicholson:

<blockquote>"You can't handle the truth!"</blockquote>

And, you know, the reality is that most folks (CPA practitioners included) *cannot* handle the truth.

When confronted by it, they wilt like a plant in the middle of the Sahara Desert – or they try to defend themselves until they are blue in the face.

I saw a great example of this a few weeks ago when I was having a conversation with a CPA who has been in business for over a decade. He was complaining about how tough things were.

I asked him what books or seminars he had recently attended, and he quickly defended himself by saying, "I don't see the need for it...not much has changed, has it?"

It was then fairly obvious to me why he was struggling. Because I believe the *opposite* to be true.

So much has changed and continues to change.

Operating a practice is very different now and what may have worked several years ago will bring dismal results today.

The reality is this:

**If your practice is *not* constantly reinventing itself,
then survival is going to be very tough.**

If your practice is not growing, it is dying. And to keep growing, you need a constant process of reinvention.

Here's a simple example of what I mean. This scenario applies to a whole range of services that CPAs offer.

With the advent of QuickBooks several years back, many CPAs saw their write-up work dramatically decline as their clients started taking their accounting in-house.

To make matters worse, the client would give the CPA their QuickBooks file after the year was over – and it would be in a state of total disarray.

So, in addition to losing revenues from write-up services, many practices faced extra work to sort this out. But, of course, the business owner would not know the mess they had made and didn't expect an invoice for the clean up.

So most CPA firms ended up losing revenue while the business owner also lost out because they had been working with an inaccurate set of books all year long.

> **GENIUS CPA**
>
> The Genius CPA knows that a practice that is not growing is dying and so follows a process of constant reinvention.
>
> **INSIGHT**

Facing the Truth

Yet, at the same time, a handful of CPA firms – like mine – saw this coming and we instituted an ongoing and paid QuickBooks Health Check service throughout the year.

So here is *the truth...*

- The truth is that if you want success for your practice, you've got to be open to change. It begins by being *curious* and asking yourself what is working, what is not, and then actively working to fix what is not working.

- The truth is if you are not squarely looking at what is not working and fixing it, you are abdicating your primary responsibility as owner and leader of your practice (and this is a big mistake).

- The truth is that the willingness to change and to reinvent is absolutely necessary.

- The truth is it will only get worse. With job losses in corporate America, there are more CPA firms starting up now than ever before. Competition is intense and it will get even more so.

There is work that needs to be done. Start by taking account of what is not working, then go at it!

The good news is that change for anyone *begins* with a decision…the decision to change things!

This decision is instantaneous – it happens in a split-second. It can happen to you *now*, as you read this.

**The decision you must make is that your future will look
very *different* from your past.**

Once that decision is made that old adage kicks in: When the student (you) is ready, the teacher (resources) will appear.

For example, one such resource is this book that you hold in your hands right now.

As you adopt this new mindset of being open to change, you will find yourself stumbling across other valuable and life-changing resources.

The key is to be ready to make some changes in the way you are used to thinking and working.

The Lesson of Change

If you have been in practice for a while, tried several things that didn't work, had your share of setbacks, and need some inspiration to climb over the fence, let me share with you the story of T. Boone Pickens.

From a mere $2,500 investment, Pickens built Mesa Petroleum, one of the largest independent oil companies in the U.S. At the age of 68, he was forced to leave Mesa Petroleum after a downward spiral in company profits.

What followed for him was a painful divorce, clinical depression, and the loss of 90 percent of his capital – but he was far from out.

From these personal and professional setbacks, he made the greatest comeback, and turned his investment fund's remaining $3 million into $8 *billion* in just a few years.

This feat made him, at age 77, the world's second-highest paid hedge fund manager.

You can read his full autobiography entitled: *The First Billion Is the Hardest: Reflections on a Life of Comebacks and America's Energy Future.*

The big lesson he taught us is that whatever has happened in your past, it is never too late to change successfully.

 **Make a commitment to** *change* **now.**

2. ESTABLISHING A CLEAR "STRATEGIC OBJECTIVE"

One of my mentors for the past fifteen years has been Stephen Covey, author of the bestselling book *The 7 Habits of Highly Effective People*.

His ideas were instrumental in helping me turn my practice from struggling to highly successful.

I clearly remember getting his audio cassette series (it makes me feel old by saying cassette tapes and not CDs) many years ago. I listened to it so frequently that the tapes got worn out to a point that the reels of a couple actually broke!

I still have them, despite the condition they are in, because of sentimental value and as a reminder of my tough journey in the early years.

One of the seven habits that Stephen identifies is "To Begin with the End in Mind."

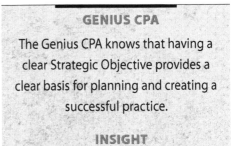

GENIUS CPA

The Genius CPA knows that having a clear Strategic Objective provides a clear basis for planning and creating a successful practice.

INSIGHT

What he means by this is that being able to create a clear picture of where you want to go will help you get there much faster and more easily.

It's rather like embarking on any journey to an unfamiliar destination. Imagine you were driving to Alaska for the first time. Without a map or clear directions, you'd end up taking many wrong turns or driving in circles for hours and perhaps not even getting there at all.

It may seem a fairly obvious error. But that's the way many CPAs attempt to run their practices or their careers. They have no clear picture of their desired destination and no map of how they plan to get there.

The end results can be the same – a great deal of wasted time and even failing to get where they want to go.

I know that when I set up my practice fifteen years ago, I had very vague ambitions such as "I want to be successful" or "I will provide good service." I might even have been a little more specific and said, "My practice will generate revenues of $2 million."

However, the truth is that I wasn't clear in my own mind about what I was trying to create. So, at that stage, the possibility of it becoming a reality was fairly slim.

It was only when I learned the power of having a Strategic Objective that I was able to create a game plan to get me there.

A Strategic Objective can serve as a clear picture of your desired destination and can be your road map for getting there.

A Strategic Objective is a one-page document that describes your practice at its best and addresses the following *big* questions:

- This is who we are.

- This is how we operate.

- This is who we serve.

- This is our competitive advantage.

To create your Strategic Objective, you need to sit down and develop a clear vision of where you want to go with your practice. Envision in your mind exactly what it will be like at some stage in the future – perhaps three, five, or ten years down the road.

Creating the first draft will take you a few hours and then you'll spend a bit of time over the next few days refining it.

Here are some crucial questions that will help you develop your Strategic Objective:

- What is the big picture for your practice? Think of your practice as a product and specify what the end product will look like in the future.

- Who are your employees? How many? Describe them.

- What will your gross billing be? $200,000; $500,000; $1 million; or several million dollars?

- What services will you provide?

- What types of clients will you be attracting? Geographic areas? Industries?

- What is your Unique Service Proposition (USP)? What makes you different from the competition? What is your reason for existence?

- How many days/hours will you work each week (during tax season, in the off-season)?

- What is the legacy you will leave behind?

Here are some tips for developing your Strategic Objective easily:

- Do this somewhere quiet – free from distractions.

- Dream big! Don't think about the "how" at this stage.

- Get it down on paper – start with a rough draft; don't worry about grammar or exact words for now.

- Read it out loud – does it sound like your story?

- Review and revise your draft the next day.

- Get feedback and input from key staff first then share it with the rest of your staff.

As soon as you have a clear Strategic Objective for what you want your practice to look like in the future, you will be much closer to making it a reality.

In addition, if you have – or plan to have – employees, having a clearly articulated vision helps everyone to have a common purpose and be on the same page.

In her bestselling book *Fierce Conversations*, Susan Scott calls this clear vision your "Stump Speech." She says that your stump speech must be powerful, clear and brief.

It must focus on **where** you are going, **why** you are going there, **who** is going with you, and **how** you are going to get there.

Great leaders repeatedly share their vision with their teams and with their customers.

They do this not only to convey a clear and compelling story, but also to provide such a degree of clarity that it is difficult to put a negative spin on their words.

Too often, I've seen CPAs starting out with a million dollar vision, but they become very disillusioned when it doesn't materialize as quickly as they would like. The truth is that creating a compelling vision is only the start of the process.

A Strategic Objective or vision needs to be backed up by a clear plan of action and it needs to be continually reviewed as you progress.

As time goes by, you should become more adept at articulating it, more able to identify the actions needed to make it a reality and ready to make it even bigger and bolder.

Create a Strategic Objective for your practice.

3. WORKING "ON" YOUR PRACTICE INSTEAD OF "IN" IT

One of the most important lessons that enabled me to turn around my practice was realizing that I was focusing too much of my effort and energy on the wrong things.

I believed that, as a CPA, I had to be the technical expert and I was spending an inordinate amount of my time doing tasks such as accounting work, preparing tax returns, and performing analyses.

The big "Aha!" moment for me was when Michael Gerber – author of *The E-Myth* series – explained the difference between working *in* your practice and working *on* your practice.

You work in your practice when you get bogged down in all of the day-to-day operational and technical tasks.

The fact is that CPAs who spend their time working in their practices have nothing more than a job. And they have a job where they are probably being underpaid for the hours they have to work.

Believe me; I know that all too well. That way of working led me along the road to high debt, low-paying clients, and a seventy-hour work week just to make ends meet.

Of course, as accounting and tax professionals, we need to have the technical knowledge and we need to be on top of the work our firms are doing for our clients. Producing quality and accurate work that meets the highest standards is extremely important.

But if we want to build a truly successful practice, we need to focus our efforts on "practice

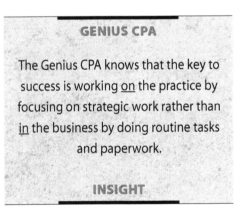

GENIUS CPA

The Genius CPA knows that the key to success is working <u>on</u> the practice by focusing on strategic work rather than <u>in</u> the business by doing routine tasks and paperwork.

INSIGHT

owner" activities such as bringing in new clients, hiring top-quality people, and creating effective systems that lead to a more efficient way of working.

Making that mental shift from working in your practice – doing day-to-day tasks – to working on the practice – doing more strategic work – is absolutely vital if you plan on taking it to the next level.

I don't think I would be too off the mark if I said that over 99% of CPA practitioners never make the mental leap from "I provide accounting services for a living" to "I market my CPA practice for a living."

The CPA practitioner "doer" sees his or her role of providing tax and accounting services as their primary role.

The Genius CPA practitioner is more marketing-minded and recognizes that their primary role is in "strategic work," which is the highest paid activity. As the owner of your practice, this is where you should be focusing your energy.

Strategic work is work that involves:

- Client acquisition

- Client retention

- Maximizing total client value

These three tasks provide a handy way of thinking about whether or not you're spending your time wisely – working on your practice – and whether you're doing all you can to grow your practice.

If you take some time to evaluate what you're doing to acquire new clients, retain current clients, and maximize your total client value, you can determine whether or not you need to shift your energy.

It can also help you evaluate the importance of any initiative or task you're considering. If the change doesn't help you in one of these three areas, is it really worth spending resources on?

Remember, money isn't your only resource. Time (yours and your employees') is just as valuable. Once I realized that I wasn't focusing enough time to work "on" the practice, I started paying more attention to it and I began to see significant changes.

So, if marketing is one of the most important strategic activities, how much time should be allocated to this in the course of a day or week?

My recommendation is to start with one to two hours per day on marketing (which equates to five to ten hours per week).

From there, it will depend on the level of growth that you desire, but that's a really good start.

 **Identify how much of your time each week you are spending on strategic tasks that help build your practice; then identify the tactical tasks you are doing that you should delegate to others.**

4. DIFFERENTIATING YOURSELF FROM THE COMPETITION

When I see CPA firms struggling, I usually find that one of their biggest problems is that they don't stand out from their competitors. There is no differentiation.

However, perhaps an even bigger concern is that many don't even see the need to differentiate themselves. They believe that having the right qualifications and offering good service is all that's necessary to prosper, but it's not.

Yet the challenges we increasingly face – such as from software programs, in-house accountants, and low-cost competitors – mean that our market is becoming more and more commoditized.

And you only need to take a quick look at the dictionary definition of "commoditization" to see why that is something you want to avoid. Here is the definition:

"The process by which a product or service reaches a point in its development where one brand has no features that differentiate it from other brands, and consumers buy on price alone."

In other words, if you do not differentiate yourself from the competition, prospective clients will only choose you because you are *cheaper* than your competitors.

Once you get into that situation, it becomes a vicious, downward spiral where people are always looking to pay less and your service will inevitably suffer as a result – never mind the effect on your profit margins.

Yet most CPAs are shooting themselves in the foot over commoditization because they:

- Say the exact same thing as their competitors.

- Try to be everything to everyone.

The Commoditization Litmus Test

Here is a simple litmus test to determine if your practice has become commoditized.

If you find yourself uttering any of the following when meeting with prospects, or using any of what follows in your marketing materials, you are a commodity.

- I have been in practice for xx years.

- We perform accounting and tax services for small business owners.

- I am a licensed CPA and have a graduate degree in accounting from ABC University.

- Client needs come first.

- We are a one-stop shop…accounting, taxes, and financial planning.

> **GENIUS CPA**
>
> The Genius CPA knows that they need to stand out from their competitors so that they don't have to compete with others purely on fees.
>
> **INSIGHT**

- We charge reasonable fees.

Be warned, this phenomenon of being perceived as a commodity is not something that the market has done to you.

You are the one who has handed over full control of the decision-making process to the prospective client by not providing any other way of allowing them to see why your firm is any different, or any better, than the many other firms vying for their business.

The fact is there are clients and prospective clients who are quite willing to pay a premium for the services they need. You just need to show them that yours is the firm that is worth the extra dollars, and that you can and will deliver.

Spouting the same old lines like "The client comes first" is a surefire way to *not* secure these valuable clients.

The Lesson of Potato Chips

Being the parent of a fourteen-year-old daughter and a nine-year-old (9½ as he often corrects me) son, our grocery shopping list usually includes a bag of potato chips among other food items that appeal to kids of that age.

After a recent visit to the supermarket, I couldn't help but notice the photo on the back of a bag of Herr's Potato Chips of the founder Jim Herr, along with.a short narration about his company's chips.

This is part of what he wrote:

> "What gives our chips their exceptional, great taste?
> It's no secret. It's the way they're made! We take special
> care to select only the finest potatoes. We cook them in
> vegetable oil so they turn out crisp and tasty and then
> quickly seal them in Herr's special foil-like packaging.
> Sunlight and moisture are locked out. Freshness is
> locked in. The result – you get more of the natural
> potato taste you crave!"

Although many other potato chip manufacturers could probably say similar things, they have created a story which makes them stand out as different.

Can you see the difference between that and the general statements I mentioned in the litmus test earlier? Can you see that it's possible to create a story about your practice that gives people a reason to choose you over the competition?

I suggest you create your own list that conveys your own personal story and uniqueness.

Asking yourself the following questions and writing down the answers can help you through the process:

- Why am I in practice?

- Why do I do what I do?

- How does my firm serve others?

- What do I sell? (Hint: it is *not* accounting and tax services.)

- What are the features and benefits of my services?

- What is/are my target market(s)? Be specific, look at all the segments of your practice to determine the niche or niches you prefer to work with.

- What are my competencies and what do I do best?

- How well do I stand out from my competition?

The end result is a core story, like Jim Herr's, which conveys a purpose and a strong reason to be a player in that industry.

Once you have your core story, it will serve you in multiple ways.

It can be developed into copy for your website; parts of it will make its way into sales letters and ads; some of it could be part of your Strategic Objective; and it could even serve as a handy list to help describe your firm to new employees.

You will find the answers to these questions very helpful as we go through the chapters on positioning, personal branding and promotion.

There is one final thought that I want to leave with you on this topic. The story must be yours and it must be true, so it's worth spending a bit of time working out what makes you special.

Develop your own core story to show what makes you different from the competition.

5. STREAMLINING YOUR PRACTICE BY CREATING EFFECTIVE SYSTEMS

If you are going to follow the "practice owner" mindset and spend more of your time on the strategic aspects of your practice, you need to be able to rely on others to carry out the practical tasks effectively.

However, gone are the days when you could recruit staff into your practice and have them stay with you for thirty or forty years.

In those days, you probably would have had employees who had built up a huge amount of knowledge that was generally stored in their heads. Everyone knew the best way to do things and, when new employees came along, the existing staff would have happily passed this on.

These days, the pace of change is such that many procedures have to change regularly and employees can move to new jobs many times during their careers.

This means that, when staff move on, they take their knowledge with them and it can take some time to get new recruits up to speed.

I'll talk in a later chapter about how you can minimize the effects of this problem by recruiting, motivating and retaining top quality staff.

However, the reality is that change is constant both in people and in procedures, so you need to be prepared.

In my experience, all the successful accounting practices I have studied have created a manual that defines how they do things – often called a "Policies and Procedures" or "Operating Procedures" manual.

They have not only defined and identified "how they do things" so that they can deliver quality services in a predictable manner, they have also documented everything so that all staff perform the same tasks in a consistent manner.

You may think this is unnecessary bureaucracy – especially if you have a small office. But there is no doubt that having well-documented systems can make it much easier to get things done quickly and to bring on new people.

If you standardize and record your procedures, everyone knows what they are and how things should be done.

If you don't have these systems in place, everything becomes dependent on you. That means that if anything happened to you – even for a short time – the practice would be thrown into chaos.

I know a CPA who unfortunately suffered from a heart attack at the height of tax season. Fortunately, he fully recovered, but he was out of commission for six weeks and lost a fair number of his clients as a result.

He had no systems in place to enable someone else to keep his office going during his absence. It took some time for his firm to recover from this setback.

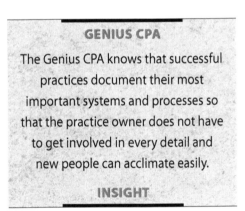

GENIUS CPA

The Genius CPA knows that successful practices document their most important systems and processes so that the practice owner does not have to get involved in every detail and new people can acclimate easily.

INSIGHT

Aside from that type of risk, establishing clear procedures fits in with the aim of taking yourself out of working in the practice. You should be spending less of your time in the mechanics of the business and more on the strategy.

Documenting systems for all the functions of your practice can make the process of delegating to your staff much smoother and more efficient. As changes happen, you can simply adjust the systems you have in place to accommodate them.

Well-documented procedures can also enhance the client's overall experience, since it makes it less likely that the client will ever be surprised by a seemingly random change in how services are delivered.

Creating Systems for Your Office

As you get started with creating systems for your office, the best advice I can offer you is to start small.

Set a goal to document, implement and monitor one process per week during tax season (or some other variation that works for you) and increase the pace during the non-tax season months.

This approach is far more practical and doable for CPA practitioners and it will keep you focused on small steps, allowing you to implement changes as you go.

You will probably find it best to organize your "how-to" processes into functional groups. In my practice, I have broken it into the following seven areas – Leadership, Marketing, Management, Money, Lead Generation, Lead Conversion, and Client Fulfillment.

There's no right or wrong way – so choose the split that works best for you.

You then need to identify all the events that occur in your practice that call for a process, such as:

- Getting a lead (or prospect).

- Getting a new client.

- Receiving a bill from a vendor.

- Hiring a new employee.

After you have selected the process you want to document, it's time to pull together all your resources such as forms, information, or checklists you currently use to complete the tasks.

TIPS ON CREATING EFFECTIVE PROCEDURES

Here are some tips on creating effective working procedures:

- Start by pulling together all the resources you currently use to complete tasks, such as checklists and forms.

- Then write out step-by-step what you actually do to complete each task.

- Add as much information as possible, but keep it simple and concise – use alphabetical and numerical listings, logical sub-headings, and bullet points.

- Create simple charts and graphics to make the processes easy to follow.

- Reference any forms or checklists needed and attach copies.

- Once you have your process finished, type it up and save it in the computer folder where you plan to keep all of them. Then print a copy and place it in a ring binder (including any supporting forms or checklists).

- Use the process as an opportunity to address any problems and issues – reward your staff for drawing attention to problems rather than covering them up.

- As the practice owner, take responsibility for the processes ensuring they are consistent with your overall vision and standards.

There is no time like the present to get started with this exercise. In fact, it is often easier to implement the processes one at a time instead of trying to make a lot of changes at once.

You can start gradually and you'll probably find it is completed much faster than you expect.

I've found that lack of documented systems is the missing piece for many practitioners.

Fixing this will enable you to build a practice that liberates you from the tyranny of daily tasks, and allows you to focus more on the strategic stuff.

 **Start identifying the key systems in your practice and begin documenting them.**

6. MAKING THE BEST USE OF YOUR TIME BY SETTING PRIORITIES

If you want to free up your time to focus on the strategic tasks that will help build your practice, you should always work on the basis that time is your most important resource.

Time is one resource that can never be recovered or replaced, but I find too many practitioners make the mistake of spending their time on the wrong tasks.

Just compare these two and consider which one is more like you:

Practitioner #1: Overworked Jackie/Jack

- Works long and hard – six or seven days per week, 70 - 80 hours per week.

- Tries to crank out as many tax returns as possible.

- Is exhausted at the end of each day. Family, social life and health take a toll.

- After tax season, finds it very difficult to jumpstart marketing because it was ignored and unattended for so long.

Practitioner #2: Visionary Vicky/Vince

- Works hard, but not as hard as Practitioner #1. Works 40 - 50 hours per week during tax season. Makes sure to take one complete day off during the weekend

- Spends half a day per week on marketing activities. Has written goals and is steadily working on accomplishing them. (Either keeps door shut or does this away from main office, e.g. library or home office.)

- Plans a short getaway in the third week of March to relax and chill out.

- Trains the staff to run the "ship" when he or she is away.

- At the completion of tax season, while other practitioners in his local area are catching their breath and in recovery mode, he or she is pumped and ready to attract more quality clients for the rest of the year.

If you find yourself a bit more like Practitioner #1, here are a few techniques that will help you become more like Practitioner #2.

TIPS ON MANAGING YOUR TIME

There is probably no skill more crucial in building a successful CPA practice than effective time management. I have found that the following secrets have worked well for me in my practice.

1. Boycott Your Phone

I don't answer the phone. Every phone call is routed through my administrative team.

They screen my calls and route them to the appropriate person. I've found that even though my phone rings, the call can often be handled by someone else in the office.

For those clients I must handle personally, I block time on my calendar to make and return phone calls between 12:30 - 1:00 PM and 4:30 - 5:00 PM during the three days that I'm in the office.

My clients know that I will respond to their calls during these times. I also direct clients to email if they require a quick response. Email is a great timesaver because I can quickly forward questions and requests to the appropriate person.

I believe this habit saves me three to four hours of time per week.

2. Respect the To-Do List

I know that to-do lists have received a bad rap lately, but I haven't found a better tool to keep me on task throughout my day. I maintain a daily, weekly, and annual list to help stay focused throughout the year.

One warning though. Don't use your to-do list as a dumping ground for miscellaneous items. Strive to use it as a tool for achieving your long-term goals.

I estimate using a to-do list effectively saves me four to six hours of time per week.

3. Organize Your Time into Blocks

Most CPAs sporadically schedule client appointments throughout their work week. This scattershot approach makes it difficult to work uninterrupted or gain momentum throughout your day.

Instead, first consider the most advantageous times to schedule your appointments for maximum efficiency.

When you cluster your appointments in batches, this allows you to handle client service, while also freeing up large blocks of focused, uninterrupted time.

Personally, I identify the things that are important, and those are blocked on my calendar. Let me give you a few examples of items that get blocked off:

- Quarterly meetings with business clients.

- Any client projects that I am working on.

- Staff meetings.

- Time assigned to marketing and meeting with prospects.

If you block off time on your calendar like this, you'll see that there is actually very little available time left. This is a great way to identify areas that are time-wasters in your schedule.

When you aggressively plug the time leaks in your schedule, you'll be surprised by how productive your day, week, month, or year becomes.

Do you realize the monetary benefit of effective time management?

Here it is: if you were, conservatively, to save ten hours per week due to the techniques that I have described here, at an average hourly rate of only $150 per hour, it would equate to an additional billable time value of $75,000.

That makes it worth investing a few minutes in planning your day, doesn't it?

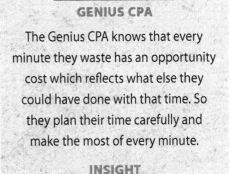

GENIUS CPA

The Genius CPA knows that every minute they waste has an opportunity cost which reflects what else they could have done with that time. So they plan their time carefully and make the most of every minute.

INSIGHT

4. Delegate with Success

I don't know what it is about CPAs that makes us such poor delegators. Perhaps it's because we are simply control freaks and don't want to let go of the technical aspects of our practice.

Or maybe it's because we believe that no one else in our firm can do it as well as we can.

Whatever the reasons, lack of delegation will get in the way of building your practice. Delegation is a prime management skill that will allow you to allocate your time and energy toward other projects. It also helps to develop employees for advancement. The best way to understand the cost of not delegating is to look at it from the standpoint of opportunity cost.

That means the real question is, what type of work are you *not* able to do because you are tied up with the technical work?

One practitioner I spoke to told me he spent most of his time doing the accounting and tax work because he was so good at this type of work that it just didn't make sense to delegate it to anyone else.

So I took him through a process of thinking about it differently.

I explained that he needed to understand the opportunity cost of being fully engaged in the accounting and tax work. This meant he did not have time to bring in new clients through teaching, speaking, and other client-generating activities that he actually loved to do.

Once he saw the opportunity cost in dollars, he brought in some help so he could devote a few mornings and evenings to speak to local groups.

When I last talked to him, he shared with me that he had already signed up a few monthly business clients thanks to his speaking activities, and that this had also rekindled his enthusiasm and energy to take his practice to the next level.

Ontario CPA Joe Truscott has also seen the benefits of taking control of his time.

"I am no longer reviewing every personal tax return that comes through my practice," he says.

He has begun by identifying some A and B clients with whom he wants to stay involved, but is transitioning to having his staff take on preparing returns for the other clients.

The next step will be having staff handle all matters for the other clients so that he is freed up to spend more time working on strategic issues and dealing with those clients with whom he wants to stay involved.

If you are ready to delegate some of your accounting and tax work, here are some tips to help you do it successfully:

- **Don't look for perfection:** Your objective is to get the job done, not create a masterpiece. Establish a standard of quality and a fair timeframe for reaching it. Once you establish your expectations, let your staff decide how to carry out the projects following the systems you create.

- **Set the parameters:** Make sure your employees have all the information needed to complete the job. Confirm that they understand and accept the requirements before you consider it delegated.

- **Focus on teaching skills:** As you hand over work tasks, it's important to understand that learning new skills sometimes includes making mistakes. Don't punish employees who make a good faith effort to do things right.

- **Check on progress:** Let the employee do the work, but check in periodically on progress. However, make sure you don't look over their shoulders or watch their every move (you don't need to be Big Brother). When you outline your expectations in the beginning, make sure you build in checkpoints for follow up. Remember to delegate work, not abdicate it.

5. Learn to Say "No"

In an effort to satisfy clients, employees and colleagues, too often we fall into the habit of agreeing to any and all requests. This may be a trait learned in childhood, when we are expected to do as we are told and we try to please our parents, teachers, and peers.

What we need to remember, as adults, is that the key to a healthy, balanced life is knowing our limits and realizing that the sheer volume of requests that we are bombarded with every day is simply unrealistic and counterproductive to success.

Of course, when deciding whether to agree to a particular request or to say "No," make sure you show consideration and ensure that you are not just refusing requests for the sake of it.

You will garner a lot of respect by striking the right balance, and will encourage others to work things out for themselves or to come up with their own solutions if you are not there to hold their hand the whole way.

6. Take a Break

You know how sometimes your computer is sluggish and won't cooperate?

When these moments strike, often your only option is to switch your PC off and reboot. The same goes for us – sometimes the brain just needs a refresh.

Slogging it out 24/7 might seem on the surface a great way to get a lot done, but the quality of your work will certainly suffer.

Paradoxically, you might find that taking an hour or two, or even the afternoon or an entire day off gives your mind a chance to relax and unwind. When you return to the task at hand you will be more focused and perform at a higher level than if you had worked on through with no respite.

These six time-management techniques will not magically create more hours in the day, but they will help you to manage your 24 hours per day more effectively.

So, if you'd like to get more done in less time, try implementing some of these tools into your daily life and you will soon see a beneficial effect on your practice and your well-being.

 **Identify several ways you can free up more time to focus on working on your practice.**

7. BECOMING EXTRAORDINARY AND CREATING A WORLD-CLASS PRACTICE

Just recently I had two very different experiences – both coincidentally involving "chairs" – that really brought home to me how small things can make or break the success of a practice.

The first was when I was in an office supply store, looking to buy an executive-style leather chair for myself.

After I tried several chairs, I picked one that seemed the most comfortable to me and I told the sales person that I would like them to assemble it for me.

There were several large signs promoting immediate onsite assembly. I am usually a klutz at any do-it-yourself type work so that was a big attraction to me!

I had already gotten the strong feeling that the salesperson did *not* want to sell me a chair. The reason I felt that was during my twenty-minute visit, he attended to two personal calls and at least one text message (okay, it may have been a tweet) on his cell phone.

However, I assumed that when I was ready to get out my credit card, he would move into action.

Instead he told me there was no one onsite who could assemble the chair that I wanted to purchase and that I should call the store the next day to find out when someone could do it. So I asked him to help me find a store that had this chair and a person onsite who could assemble it for me.

Unbelievably, he said that he wouldn't be able to do that and I should physically go to the other stores.

The end result of this experience was that I decided not to buy my chair from them, and got it from their competitor instead.

Now this guy may not have been bothered about losing that one sale, but I'll never go back there and I've told many people about my experience. Who knows how much my one bad experience has cost that store.

Yet, I had a very different experience with chairs this past Memorial Day weekend while walking around the small town of Troy in upstate New York with my family.

Passing a jewelry store, my eye caught a small sign saying "Husband Chair Inside."

My immediate thought was how considerate the owners were and that they truly understood me. So I suggested to my family that we go inside. We ended up spending several hundred dollars in there – all because my attention was caught by the three magical words on the sign.

My point in both cases is that seemingly small things matter.

In the first case, the salesman did not even pretend to take an interest in me and my needs.

In the second, the store owner thought about the needs of his customers and used that as a way to attract the attention of passing customers.

These small things make the difference between ordinary and extraordinary, between simple survival and outrageous success in a business.

I came across a quote some time ago that sums this up:

"Small Hinges Swing Big Doors."

Even the largest door will yield to a small push thanks to a couple of tiny hinges.

Have you allowed the "hinges" in your practice to seize up? Or are they a tad rusty?

Have you overlooked the little things that may seem insignificant on their own but can actually make an enormous impact – for better or worse?

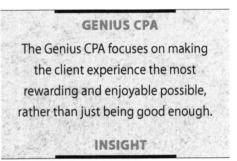

GENIUS CPA

The Genius CPA focuses on making the client experience the most rewarding and enjoyable possible, rather than just being good enough.

INSIGHT

You have to determine what extras you can deliver to give your clients the best possible experience; to enable others to see your practice as a trusted, valued, respected and expert advisor.

The way to greatness today is to transfer your concerns away from the technical aspects of the services you deliver and focus instead on the people you serve.

By doing so, you will begin to look at your practice as a whole, and you will come to see any interaction that clients have with any part of your practice as part of an overall *experience.*

I promise you this: if you strive on making it the best, most rewarding, most fulfilling, most enjoyable experience for the client, you will dominate your market place. There is no doubt in my mind about that.

Just think of how you feel as a customer when you experience particularly good or bad service.

The good news for us as practitioners is that clients' everyday experiences of customer service are, for the most part, negative. Hence, their low expectations for great service!

You can therefore surprise and delight your clients by making their experience your #1 priority. For example:

- Have a staff member respond to all inquiries within two hours.

- Send your client a business referral.

- Deliver a birthday gift for their children!

- Call them 24 hours in advance to remind them of their appointment with you.

Have fun with this. Over-delivering is where good practices become great. Where ordinary or average becomes extraordinary and world class.

One more thing that is very important – keep your eyes and ears open when you are at the office. Listen to the way your staff members talk to clients.

- Are they courteous, friendly and professional?

- Do they listen well and engage the client?

If you really want to find out what they are saying, then try "mystery shopping." This means you have someone call the office pretending to be a prospective client.

When you hear how this person is being assisted, I guarantee you will identify a need for improvement!

As the owner of your firm, it's your responsibility to assess what needs to be improved, and to provide the necessary training.

Dedicate your CPA practice to extraordinary customer service and you will quickly see the benefits. Clients will respect your fees even if they are higher than your competition.

Also, they will realize they have found a special resource and spread the stories of your services all over town!

Making Ordinary Extraordinary

As I mentioned earlier, I am a big movie fan and get to watch my fair share of films in the theaters. However I generally try to stay away from the television, other than an occasional show, as I feel TV is a big time zapper – and it simply doesn't thrill me.

However, recently my mother-in-law – with whom I get along really well – was visiting for a few days and I made an exception by watching an hour-long cooking show, "Dinner Impossible."

Being the marketing addict I am, of course I watched the show from a marketing standpoint!

If you are not familiar with this show, Chef Robert Irvine serves stunningly creative dishes for both intimate gatherings and huge crowds, all without warning and at a moment's notice.

On this episode, he has cooked on a desert island, in an 18th-century kitchen, in an ice hotel, for cowboys on a cattle drive, for master instructors at the Culinary Institute of America, and at the inauguration of Pennsylvania's governor.

What I observed as I watched the show was that, at the end of the day, it was a cooking show presented in a very interesting and *entertaining* way.

Irvine was required in this episode, to cook a gourmet, seven-course, fundraising dinner for forty-five guests who had each paid $15,000 for this meal.

The *extraordinary* key that elevated this show from just a run-of-the-mill cooking program into an intense one-hour *drama* was that he had to cook this meal in these difficult conditions:

He had only five hours to deliver; he had to cook using camping gear; there was a severe thunderstorm while he cooked; he had to catch his own fish, and one of the assistants hated to cook.

So why would the producer go to all this effort and expense? The answer is that they *must* create something extraordinary to attract the viewers and keep their interest for the entire one-hour show.

The lesson from this is that we have to ask ourselves what *extraordinary* things we are doing in our practices to get the attention of our prospects and clients?

Most practitioners don't do anything…hence the opportunity for you to use the genius insights you discover by reading this book.

A number of years ago, I stumbled across the following saying that has stayed with me ever since:

"In the land of the blind, the one-eyed man is king."

What it means for you is that you don't have to be a superstar marketer to excel in your CPA practice.

Your competitors (other CPAs) are doing such a lousy job in marketing that any improvement you make in marketing your practice will make it stand out by a mile.

To get your creative juices flowing, here is one example that I use in my practice – and it may even be right for you and your firm.

During tax season, my firm buys gifts in bulk from a wholesaler called The B & F System Inc. (www.bnfusa.com) to give away at the end of the tax return process.

When the client comes to our office to pick up their tax return, after having paid their fees – this is one of the reasons my firm has virtually zero dollars in collections for tax preparation fees – the client is encouraged to choose a gift from the assortment sitting on a shelf.

Our clients love this process. It gives the entire tax preparation process an extraordinary touch right at the end – first and last impressions are the most remembered.

Then the mention of the free gift makes an effective segue for my front office staff member to hand the client a couple of referral slips.

I'll keep coming back to this point as we go through the book – you need to stand out from the competition if you want to have the Ultimate CPA Practice.

Often it's how you do the ordinary that makes you extraordinary.

The more attention you pay to the small things, the more success you will have with the big ones.

In addition, the more you can learn about customer service, success conditioning and entrepreneurship, the more successful you will be. For starters, here are four books you *must* read:

- *Think and Grow Rich* by Napoleon Hill

- *The E-myth Re-visited* by Michael Gerber

- *Good to Great* by Jim Collins

- *Outstanding!: 47 Ways To Make Your Organization Exceptional* by John G. Miller

You should always be looking for ways to make your practice extraordinary.

By the way, you'll notice that I refer to quite a few business books. I am an avid reader of business books and devour about one book per week.

Many years back, I remember one of my mentors saying that there is no difference between a person who doesn't know how to read and one who knows how to read but will not.

I opted to be neither and now own a room full of books…they are some of my most valued possessions.

 **Find out how your employees are interacting with your clients and prospects and take whatever steps are necessary to make improvements.**

Preparing for Success:
TOP MISTAKES TO AVOID

Here are common mistakes that prevent CPA practitioners from setting up a practice that is ready to grow to its full potential:

- **Being unwilling to change.** The pace of change in our profession and in today's world is so fast that only those who keep evolving are likely to survive and thrive.

- **Lacking a Strategic Objective.** It is too easy to get bogged down in the detail of the work of your practice. You need a picture of what you want it to be like in the future to keep motivating you towards something better.

- **Having a "job" working in the practice.** Too many CPAs get absorbed in the technical aspects of their work and don't leave enough time for the important elements of building their practice.

- **Lacking systems.** Without established systems and procedures, it is difficult to delegate and you therefore struggle to find time to build the practice.

- **Wasting time.** If you are not using your time well, you will not have enough time to concentrate on making your practice better.

- **Not standing out from the competition.** Prospective clients will only want to talk about fees unless you give them another reason to choose you.

- **Failing to delegate.** Trying to do everything yourself means you don't have time for more productive work and your employees don't get the chance to develop.

- **Not setting high enough standards.** Your clients probably have lots of experience with bad service. So make your practice the exception. Over-delivering is where good practices become great.

KEYS TO SUCCESS

- Being Open to Change
  Recognizing the truth and being ready to change the way you work
  and think is the key to future success.

- Setting a Strategic Objective
  Being able to create a clear picture of where you want to go will help
  you get there much faster and more easily.

- Working On Your Practice
  The mental shift from working in your practice to working on the
  practice is absolutely vital.

- Standing Out from the Competition
  Having a reason why prospects should choose your practice instead
  of a competitor is crucial to its success.

- Creating Systems
  Successful practices have a manual that defines the systems and
  processes for how they do things.

- Setting Priorities
  There is arguably no more important resource than time, as it's
  one thing that can never be recovered or replaced, so it's crucial to
  manage it carefully.

- Becoming World Class
  As a CPA practitioner, you have to develop the mindset of seeing
  your practice as a product. Surprise and delight your clients by
  making the quality of their experience your #1 priority.

Make a note of the additional key points from this chapter and what
actions you are going to take as a result.

2
POSITIONING AND PLANNING:

Standing Out from the Competition to Become First Choice in Your Market

----

*"Positioning is not what you do to a product.
Positioning is what you do
to the mind of the prospect."*

AL RIES AND JACK TROUT
AUTHORS: *POSITIONING: THE BATTLE FOR YOUR MIND*

VIRTUALLY ALL PRACTITIONERS, no matter what services they provide, make two crippling mistakes when marketing:

1. They say the exact same thing as their competitors; and

2. They try to be everything to everyone.

In the previous chapter, I shared with you something I refer to as the "commoditization litmus test"…a simple test to determine if your practice has become commoditized.

I mentioned that you will know you are commoditized when you hear yourself uttering things such as how long you have been in practice, listing the qualifications you have, detailing the services you offer, or making vague statements such as "the client comes first."

The big *danger* when everyone looks the same and sounds the same is that the only way for your would-be clients to differentiate one firm from another is by fees.

As I shared before, price shopping and commodity pricing *aren't* things the market does to you. They're something *you* unknowingly do to yourself by virtue of having nothing unique to say, no message that communicates to your ideal client that, "Yes, my firm is what you're looking for."

The truth is, most clients are willing to pay premium fees for things they desperately want. They just don't know if yours is the business that is worth the fees. *So you have to tell them.*

In this chapter, I'll be explaining how you can find a way to position your practice so that it stands out from the competition.

I'll also talk about how you can communicate that positioning effectively so that your ideal prospects start contacting you. Later, we'll look in more detail about the strategies you can use for getting that message across.

However, it's crucial to take a step back and approach this strategically before rushing into marketing tactics.

To develop a successful marketing strategy, you need to master the 3M's of marketing:

- Market: Who buys your services.

- Message: Why they buy from you.

- Media: How you get your message across to them.

Most CPAs don't take the time to work through each of these elements and few understand that the sequential order of looking at them is very important. That's why so many practitioners have problems with their marketing.

They end up buying advertising based on which ad rep calls them the most, or they spend a fortune running ads that have no clear message.

The key to getting this right is that you must work through them in the order just mentioned.

You must begin the process with a good picture of your ideal clients; then define a clear message to communicate with this group and finally decide which media you want to use to get it across.

It's important to get all three elements right, as having one of them out of order causes problems with the other two. I cannot emphasize this enough.

The incorrect order would result in a great message being wasted if you deliver it to the wrong market. Equally, choosing the wrong media will mean you don't reach the market you are looking for or you will spend far too much on getting it across.

That's why time invested at this stage can pay great dividends as you work through the other stages in the chapters that follow.

The "heavy lifting" work of clearly identifying your market and message may not be as sexy (or fun or easy) as the later aspects of the marketing process, such as creating your marketing materials or choosing the media.

But once these steps have been completed, the other steps become easier and you get considerably better results.

DEFINING YOUR MARKET — THE "WHO"

The first step in the process of developing your strategy is getting a clear picture of your target market.

In an increasingly competitive world, practitioners are looking at ways to maximize their revenue and it can often seem that the best path to higher profits is to appeal to as many people as possible. But the reality is that this rarely pans out.

There are several reasons why finding your ideal market and focusing on them is important:

- When you focus on a specific market, you are more likely to be seen as an authority. Experts can charge higher fees (for example, heart surgeons command a higher fee than general practitioners), attract more clients, and are more sought after by the media.

- Having a clear picture of your market makes it much easier to find your ideal clients – you know where they hang out, what magazines they read, and what services they are looking for.

- Choosing who you want to work with makes your firm more rewarding and pleasant – you can select the types of personalities that you most enjoy being around.

There are two factors to take into account when defining your market:

- Demographics

- Psychographics

Demographics includes all the *factual* and *quantifiable* information about your market – where they are based, age group, market sector, size of business, gender, etc.

Psychographics tells you more about *what they are like* – type of personality, interests, and lifestyles.

Let me give you an example of demographics by looking at my practice's client list. Most of my clients fall into one or more of the following groups:

- Businesses with revenues of $1 million – $10 million, with up to fifty employees and within ten miles of my office.

- Dentists within ten miles of my office.

- Chiropractors and wellness practices within ten miles of my office.

- Service professionals within ten miles of my office (except medical doctors and attorneys).

When you look at the psychographics, you would find that many of them are down to earth, friendly, respectful of my time and caring about my well-being. They recognize that working with me and my firm is crucial for their success and they pay my practice for the high value that we bring to the table.

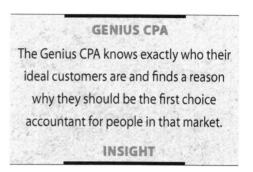

GENIUS CPA

The Genius CPA knows exactly who their ideal customers are and finds a reason why they should be the first choice accountant for people in that market.

INSIGHT

The thing is, I was not that clear about this in my early years in practice. I had clients in all types of industries and of all sizes – including really tiny start-ups – because I was trying to be all things to all people.

If someone was prepared to pay my fees – which were painfully low at that time – I would sign them up even if they were blatantly rude or had a bad attitude during my initial meeting with them.

The end result was that my practice had a large number of low-paying, demanding and unappreciative clients that my staff and I had to deal with every day.

Of course, the attributes I now look for in my ideal client may not be exactly the right ones for you. It will depend on your background, your area, the competition and your priorities. You have to work through this process yourself.

That's exactly the process that Florida Superstar member Mayumi Todd, CPA, went through to take her practice from having three clients – and working from the kitchen table – to building a team looking after more than 350 clients.

She started out following the traditional approach of networking by joining chambers and business associations. She realized she was struggling to stand out from the competition and was being put off by the number of rejections she was receiving.

The turning point for her was discovering that, being Japanese, she could offer services to Japanese business owners that her competitors could not as easily provide.

Most of those business owners were not using a Japanese accountant, but they hesitated to contact their American accountant when they had broader questions about business, wealth, taxes, or visas.

When she started conversations with them, they asked many questions not only about taxes and accounting, but on more general issues as well. She was even providing translation services for them.

By deciding to focus on this specific group of clients, she was not only able to build a bigger practice, she found it more enjoyable and rewarding.

"My next goals are to reach seven figures and be able to spend more time with my family," she says.

Clearly each of us has our own relevant skills and experience. The key is to identify what specific expertise or way of working you offer – or can introduce – that will make you the obvious choice for people in your target market.

FINDING YOUR IDEAL CLIENTS

In order to identify your ideal clients, you need to be able to define them according to the demographics and psychographics.

Here are some factors you need to take into account in identifying your ideal clients:

- **Existing clients:** Start by finding out as much as possible about your existing client base. Dig into your records and add more insights based on what you know about them. The people you currently do business with may not be your ideal clients, but it is a useful starting point. For example, you may identify one segment within the total that may be suitable to build on.

- **Competition:** Look at the strengths and weaknesses of your competitors and what they are offering. Are there any obvious gaps in the market or are there any areas where everybody looks the same and you can offer something different? Contrary to popular belief, you should never be scared of competition in a healthy market. The existence of competitors is a strong indication that there is demand.

- **Expertise:** Consider your own personal expertise and that of other people in your practice. Often this suggests a market area that might be appropriate. You may have particular advantages in a certain industry such as relevant skills, knowledge, or contacts.

- **Earning potential:** Take into account the earning potential from this market. You don't want to define your ideal market in a territory where there are not enough clients willing to pay decent fees.

- **Growth prospects:** Think about the future. Does this market offer potential for future growth and, if you grow, will you be able to recruit the right quality staff to meet the needs of this particular market?

- **Ease of contact:** You want to choose markets that are easily accessible, e.g., because people all hang out in the same place or you can reach them through mailing lists or advertising.

The key to this process is to define in detail the kind of people you want to do business with.

When you develop this definition, bear in mind that you are not setting cast-iron rules about who you will do business with. You are defining your ideal prospects so that you can target them more effectively with your marketing.

For example, I'm not going to turn away a potential client just because they are based fifteen miles from my office. But I'm probably not going to advertise in their local paper.

Even if you already have a successful, established practice, it is always beneficial to go through this exercise. It may help you identify new niches you previously hadn't thought of, or highlight opportunities you are missing.

In this process, you want to be as specific as possible. Note their age, sex, income group, and even where they live, if it impacts your practice. Note their industries, number of employees, and revenues. Look for patterns and identify the groups that are most appropriate.

When you think about psychographics, identify the kind of people you want to deal with. I mentioned above some of the factors that matter to me. I suggest that you draw up your own list of the attributes of the kind of people you want to work with. For example, you may choose to list factors such as:

- Happily give us referrals.

- Value what we do for them.

- Are fun to work with.

- Readily pay our fees on time.

- Respond to information requests quickly.

In addition to identifying those groups you want to do business with, you also need to be clear about the types or groups of people you *don't* want to work with. This may be a personal choice or it may have to do with the skills in your practice.

For example, I don't like working with either medical doctors or attorneys. My experiences with these two groups have led me to believe that many of the folks within each of these two groups are pompous and difficult to deal with!

Simply, medical doctors and lawyers just don't fit my "ideal client" profile of being down to earth, respectful, etc. I feel that my staff and I are happier when we have no medical doctors or attorneys on our client roster.

Now that is my choice and it means that, for someone else who thinks differently, there is a potentially attractive niche dealing with medical doctors and attorneys in my area.

My coaching member John Hemmendinger, a New Jersey based CPA, has a very different view and has many positive experiences of dealing with physicians and attorneys.

He has found that being able to define and articulate the kind of clients he wants to go after is a big time saver.

As he only works with professional practices in certain fields, he does not waste time getting up to speed on new areas.

He concentrates only on working in markets where he knows the issues and can give great assistance to those clients.

This approach gives him a lot more productive time. "It means I am not spending ten hours doing something that should really take me only five."

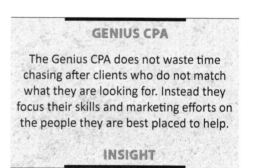

GENIUS CPA

The Genius CPA does not waste time chasing after clients who do not match what they are looking for. Instead they focus their skills and marketing efforts on the people they are best placed to help.

INSIGHT

The key point is that, overall, you have to resist the impulse to serve anyone and everyone.

You've heard the old saying "You can't be all things to all people." Remember this every time you're tempted to try to market yourself to everyone.

If you want to establish yourself as an expert in a certain industry or type of service, and are selective as to the personality and character types of people you enjoy working with, then I urge you to start the marketing process by defining a clear market and giving this step the time and attention it warrants.

 **Define the demographic and psychographic details of your ideal clients, taking into account the above factors.**

ESTABLISHING A CLEAR MESSAGE—THE "WHY"

When you have defined your ideal target market, you then need to establish a clear message that shows prospects *why* they should do business with you.

It is critical to explain to them why they should choose you over the competition – in fact, if you have clear positioning in the right market, the entire process leading from prospect to client becomes a whole lot easier.

If you can demonstrate that you are the best person to solve their problem, they will gladly hire you.

That's why it's so important to define your market *before* you create the message. The message has to respond to the problems and concerns of your target market and you can only create it effectively when you know enough about the market.

For example, when Mayumi Todd identified that she was going to focus on working with Japanese clients, you can see how much easier it was for her to craft a marketing message.

She was no longer just another accountant; she was now someone who could offer a highly targeted message for Japanese clients.

So, if your message is going to attract clients, you need to be really clear about who your target audience is, what their particular struggles or problems are right now, and how working with you solves their problems.

Then you need to be able to identify something your target clients care about that separates you from your competitors in their eyes. To come up with something that makes you stand out, you need to ask yourself questions like these:

- How is your firm different from other practices offering similar services?

- What makes you stand out from the many similar firms your prospect has to choose from?

- If you were a prospective client, what would you think was your firm's biggest strength?

There are many factors you could identify that can form part of a marketing message which makes you stand out, and you need to decide what works best for you. However, examples of factors that can serve as part of your message include:

- Unique way of working – such as working in a client's office.

- Focusing on a set market sector – such as dentists, retailers, restaurant owners, etc.

- Guaranteed timescale – such as three-day turnaround.

- Added-value services – such as pre-engagement analysis and follow-up consultations.

- Endorsement – such as from a professional body or trade association.

- Resource center – such as the ability to tap into your network of professionals.

Bear in mind that this is not simply about crafting a message. You may actually need to redefine the services you offer and make changes to the way you work to satisfy the needs of your ideal market.

By the way, you'll notice that this list does not include "price." Competing on price or fees sends exactly the wrong message to prospective clients and only encourages them to ask for further discounts.

While you need a message that stands out, it doesn't matter if you are basing your message on something that other practices offer.

It may even be something you have been doing for years. If it solves your client's problem and no-one else is specifically promoting it from that perspective, it can be part of your message.

DEFINING WHAT MAKES YOU STAND OUT

Think about the factors in your practice that your clients comment on most. Take into account the reasons people have chosen to work with you before.

What makes you special or unique?

What specific benefits do your clients get from working with you?

You should focus more on the *benefits* that clients enjoy and not the *features* of the service you deliver.

For example, if you are known for being proactive and identifying and solving problems before the situation becomes a crisis, the benefit to your clients is that they can be confident that they won't be faced with an emergency of some kind.

> **GENIUS CPA**
>
> The Genius CPA does not try to be all things to all people. They know exactly who their ideal clients are and have a clear message about why these clients should do business with them.
>
> **INSIGHT**

They can feel secure knowing that small matters will be taken care of before they become huge problems.

Do you perform services on time, every time – without fail? The benefit of this to your clients is that they can be confident that work will be completed reliably; they know they can depend on your timeframes.

Do you always complete work within the stated budget? The benefit for your clients is that they don't have to worry about unexpected costs – a valid concern for many.

As a starting point for developing your marketing message, clearly identify those features of your practice that provide benefits to your clients.

Now write down what those benefits are – not in dull, technical jargon, but in terms that a potential client would understand, identify with, and appreciate.

These benefits are the added value you provide, and what makes you different from the firm around the corner.

You should be proud of these things; they are the differentiating factors that entice a prospective client to choose your practice over all others!

When you are developing your marketing message, don't forget to incorporate what you *want* to be known for.

Example A:

Jones CPAs prepare our monthly financial statements and year-end tax filings.

Example B:

Jones CPAs play an instrumental role in maximizing the cash flow and profitability of our business. We can't imagine operating our business without them.

I don't know about you, but I think the second one has that "wow" factor. Jones CPAs have created a marketing message that tells the world they are making a significant difference for the people they serve.

Sometimes you'll find that your message establishes itself pretty quickly. Other times you will have to try a few different approaches until you get the message right. It may take a bit of work and some soul searching.

When you have identified the message that seems right for you, you need to be able to express it in words so that it grabs attention and is meaningful to the prospective clients.

It's a good idea to get direct feedback from clients and suggestions from everyone in the office before making a final decision.

However, the fact that it's not easy is the reason most practices – and most businesses – don't bother with it.

**You'll find that creating a clear marketing message is
a critical key to success.**

When you have the right message, you can use it in all your communication and marketing. It will help prospects see how you can help them and makes your marketing much more effective.

Create a clear marketing message showing why prospects should choose your practice rather than a competitor.

CHOOSING THE RIGHT MEDIA — THE "HOW"

When you have completed the first two steps, you need to choose the best ways to get your message across.

The big mistake many CPAs make is placing too much emphasis on only one form of promotion and marketing.

These days there is an ever-growing range of options for getting your message across, but it's important to do it strategically. Now that you know your ideal market, the decision about which media to use is much easier.

You can narrow down your choice significantly based on where you will find your ideal target audience. For example, if you have chosen your market based on geographic considerations, it will allow you to focus on media which operate in that area.

Equally, if you are targeting a particular group of people such as chiropractors, there are specialist media you can use to reach them. When you know your audience, it is also much easier to buy more targeted mailing lists.

So the important task at this stage is to identify venues where your target market can be found. Where you could reach them in significant numbers – the golf club, Rotary, charity events, specialist publications, online forums, local radio stations?

Start by brainstorming where you will find them.

It's a great idea to put your best effort into things you know work – such as word-of-mouth marketing, networking, or referrals. But it's a bad idea to put all your eggs in one basket.

To build a successful practice, you need to develop several marketing avenues to bring in leads.

In the rest of this book, I'll be sharing a whole range of marketing strategies and media you can use to get your message across.

It is usually best to focus on one at a time so that you can master that one before moving on to the next – but it's much better to have a range of options available.

If you want to bring in twenty new quality business clients, it is better to have five media that bring in four clients each rather than depending on one to deliver all twenty. This allows you to have a broader base and to test out new approaches.

Here are just some of the marketing media available to you:

- Direct mail

- Networking groups

- Magazine ads

- Social networking online

- Google AdWords

- Press releases

- Writing articles

- Speaking engagements

We'll be looking at all of these in more detail later. The key at this stage is to think about the special places where you can find your ideal target clients. Here are some questions to get you thinking:

- Where do they congregate?

- What do they read?

- What workshops or seminars would they go to?

- What trade shows will they attend this year?

- Where do they network?

- What clubs or organizations do they visit?

- What associations do they belong to?

- What newsletters do they read?

- What organization or group holds a list of these people?

- Where can you reach them in large numbers and affordably?

Narrow the choices down to draw up a list of the best media to reach your target market and, as we go through the rest of the book, we'll work on implementing it.

 **Identify the best ways of reaching the target market that you have defined.**

Positioning and Planning:
TOP MISTAKES TO AVOID

Here are common mistakes that cause practitioners to develop ineffective marketing messages:

1. **Not defining the market clearly enough.** Many practices make the mistake of trying to be all things to everybody and this makes it difficult for them to establish a clear position in any market.

2. **Using a label as your description.** It's not enough to have a label – "Jim Smith, CPA." You need to focus on the benefit you offer the client, such as saving them tax dollars.

3. **Being self-serving.** People don't care how big your practice is or how long you have been in business: "The largest CPA in Oldtown." Marketing messages that focus on you don't help you to differentiate yourself and can come across as outright bragging. Think about what the client is looking for in a CPA and use that.

4. **Making your message too complicated.** You want your message to be easy to remember. If it tries to say too much, no one will remember it and it will also be less believable.

5. **Making your message too short.** While your marketing message needs to be brief, it also has to be long enough to convey a benefit that is meaningful. If you say, "We are here to solve all your problems," that could mean anything. It has to come across clearly to your audience so that they know what you have to offer.

6. **Being too generic.** Good communication is specific. Vague statements like "save time" or "quick results" don't work as well as specific statements. If you can save someone time or money by the way you work, state how much.

7. **Choosing the wrong media.** You can get everything else right in your marketing and then make the mistake of choosing the wrong media to get your message across. This not only wastes money but can end up destroying the impact of your message.

KEYS TO SUCCESS

- The three key elements of marketing are:
  - Market
  - Message
  - Media

- Defining your market means identifying your ideal clients, their key attributes, and where you can find them. Aim to find an area where you can stand out – don't try to be everything for everyone.

- Establishing a clear marketing message means writing a statement making clear why people in your target market should deal with you rather than a competitor. Do this taking into account what you know your market needs and wants.

- Choosing the right media is about identifying the best way to get your message across to your target market. Take time to identify where and how you can reach your target market.

Make a note of the additional key points from this chapter and the actions you are going to take as a result.

3
PERSONAL BRANDING:

Establishing Yourself As An Expert So That Prospects and Clients Start Contacting You

----

"Your brand is what people say about you when you are not in the room."

JEFF BEZOS
FOUNDER, AMAZON.COM

ONE OF THE MOST POWERFUL ways to build your practice – or your career – is to develop a strong personal brand where you are recognized as an expert in a specific area.

This is important regardless of whether you are the owner of your practice or work as a professional in one.

Even when you have followed the steps in the previous chapter to build a strong positioning for your practice, people buy "other people" and you need to give clients and prospects a reason to have personal confidence in *you*.

I see that most CPAs don't do a good job of differentiating themselves from others. Using the personal branding process and strategies I will share with you in this chapter will help you to achieve that.

Often they hesitate to push themselves forward due to natural reticence or feeling that promoting themselves as individuals is not very professional.

But the reality is that just having a bachelor's or master's degree, a CPA license, and experience does *not* make you different from the other CPAs that the prospect is talking to.

The prospect will assume, "Hey, if someone's a CPA, they are competent to do the job well, so let me see which CPA can do it for the lowest fees."

On the other hand, if you have a strong personal brand, they see a reason to come to you.

The best and most powerful way to brand yourself is by becoming an expert.

When you are seen as an expert, "education-based marketing" can be utilized – for example through articles, speaking and special reports – that not only establishes your expertise but also makes prospects and clients more likely to seek you out.

For instance, one of the steps that helped me create real success for my practice was that I developed a reputation as the small business expert in New Jersey. I'll talk more about the steps I took to do that later in this chapter.

As soon as I started taking action to position myself as an expert – whether through my writing, speaking or special reports – owners of small businesses in my area began to contact me for advice.

Instead of me going after them, they were *pursuing* me because they saw me as a recognized expert.

There are three steps you need to follow to create a strong personal brand:

1. Identify your specific field of expertise.

2. Choose the tools you want to use to promote your expertise.

3. Leverage everything for maximum benefit.

Let's look at these three steps in more detail.

IDENTIFYING YOUR SPECIFIC FIELD OF EXPERTISE

Defining your personal brand – and choosing your field of expertise – flows on from the process of deciding your practice's target market and marketing message.

For example, as I mentioned in the last chapter, my ideal clients are small businesses in the $1 million – $10 million range. This helped me determine that the way to capture their attention was to become seen as an expert in small businesses.

The reality is there are many accountants in your area exactly like you. So you need to define an area of expertise that makes you stand out and makes potential clients want to deal with you rather than anyone else.

It goes without saying that you cannot be an expert on everything so you need to find a field that is relevant to your target market and is one where you can be seen as the expert.

The segment you choose has to be big enough to appeal to a large group of people. But it has to be narrow enough for you to be perceived as an expert.

A great example from outside our industry is Gary Vaynerchuck. He transformed his family liquor store business into a $45-million enterprise by educating himself about wine and positioning himself as the resident wine expert.

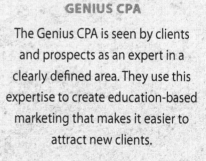

GENIUS CPA

The Genius CPA is seen by clients and prospects as an expert in a clearly defined area. They use this expertise to create education-based marketing that makes it easier to attract new clients.

INSIGHT

By promoting himself consistently in that way through various media, such as daily podcasts, he established a clear and strong personal brand that helped build his business.

He established his expertise in a way that was relevant to potential customers and made them more likely to buy from him.

Gary is by no means the only wine expert out there, but his careful positioning and constant promotion enabled him to build a strong and effective brand.

Your challenge is to find a field in your market that you can dominate in the same way.

Your personal brand may reflect the type of clients you serve or the way you work. It can be related to the types of services you offer or it may be broader.

For example, as I am seen as a small business expert, I talk about issues of interest to owners of small businesses. These issues could just as easily be their marketing concerns as their tax problems.

You may prefer to create a brand around particular services your practice offers or clients you work with. For example, if you work with many dentists, you could position yourself as an expert for dentists and perhaps other healthcare professionals.

Many people fear that being perceived as an expert in one area restricts their market. They want to appeal to as many people as possible. The truth is if you try to appeal to everyone, there is nothing that makes you stand out.

Being perceived as an expert in a specific area doesn't prevent you from working with people over your full range of services. However being seen as an expert makes it much easier for you to stand out from the competition and attract clients.

The key to establishing a strong personal brand is defining an area where you want to be seen as the expert.

You then use your field of expertise as the basis for your marketing and promotion.

Through education-based marketing, you are seen as providing useful information and valuable service rather than pushing your services or coming across as "salesy."

 **Define the area of expertise where you want to establish your personal brand.**

CHOOSING THE BEST TOOLS TO PROMOTE YOUR EXPERTISE

Once you've defined the area where you wish to be seen as the expert, there are many tools you can use to promote your brand. I cover twelve of them here.

I know that many practitioners look at this list and get intimidated – perhaps by the sheer number of options to choose from or because they feel they don't have the requisite skills to use them.

For example, it is very common for CPAs to say they can't write or they don't like speaking in public. But when you don't feel you have the right skills you can usually call for help from others.

If you hate to write, maybe you have someone on your team who is a good writer who can help you with this, or you can hire a freelancer to get you started.

However, you'll probably find that writing a few articles, for example, is much easier than you think. Remember you're not handing them in to your high school English teacher. You simply need to get some useful information across to your target clients.

I strongly encourage you to make a start using one or two of the tools and techniques I cover here. As you start to see results, and master the approaches you begin with, you will feel more comfortable about adding more strategies later.

You will get much better results by focusing on one or two at a time rather than trying to learn how to get the best results from all the approaches at once.

Here are the twelve tools:

1. WHITE PAPERS AND SPECIAL REPORTS

One of the best ways to begin establishing your personal brand is to write a special report or white paper on a topic of interest to your market.

A simple way to get started is to identify some key problems that many people in your target market face. For example, if your target market is small business owners, it could be problems with cash flow, record keeping, or paying too much tax.

For the problem you choose, identify a number of common questions that people ask or typical problems they face in that specific area. Then write a few paragraphs giving them answers to these questions or helping them deal with these problems.

The report does not have to be lengthy and can be kept to only a few pages. Be sure to give it an appealing title such as:

- 7 Ways Business Owners Can Save Tax

- 5 Secrets of Improving Your Cash Flow

You then simply need to make sure it is laid out nicely and converted into PDF format. Most word processing software now allow you to make it look good without having to pay a designer.

If you want a second opinion or feel your writing skills are not your strength, you can employ an editor to tidy it up and possibly add extra content. There are plenty of high quality writers and editors who will do this at a reasonable fee.

One good resource for finding freelance writers and editors is elance.com.

When you have your special report, you are now an author!

Authors are automatically seen as experts and this is a good start for building your personal brand.

You can use this report as an incentive for people to sign up for your email list or you can use it to support an event where you are the speaker.

This is one of the most valuable of the branding tools because it can be created very easily and can be used in so many different ways.

2. PUBLIC SPEAKING

Most CPAs hate speaking in public and avoid any invitation to do it. That's why it provides such a great opportunity for those who are willing to stand up and talk. There is usually quite a demand for interesting speakers on the topics that most CPAs can cover.

Being willing to talk to an audience – whether it's a few people at a local club or hundreds at a major seminar or conference – is an obvious way of positioning yourself as someone with expertise.

> **Speaking to an audience is a way of sharing information and generating interest in what you offer.**

You can make the process easy by creating a short presentation and delivering it over and over again with slight variations to different audiences.

The key to speaking successfully is ensuring you have a way to turn your audience's interest into follow-up meetings with targeted potential clients.

The solution for people who are nervous about speaking in public is two-fold:

- **Preparation:** If you take steps to carefully plan what you're going to say and you know your subject well, there is no reason to hold back.

- **Practice:** The more often you give your presentation, the more confident you will become.

Many people find it helpful to join speakers clubs and organizations like Toastmasters – just like I did many moons ago – in order to build experience in a more comfortable environment.

When you have spoken to a group on a particular topic, they will automatically see you as the expert on that topic and there is a very good chance that a number of them will want to follow up with you.

3. PRESS RELEASES

When you establish yourself as a recognized expert in a particular area, you will find that the media will contact you for opinions on relevant issues.

> **As with many areas of personal branding, the fact that you were quoted in the media establishes you in other people's eyes as a genuine expert.**

For example, I was recently featured on the cover of *Accounting Today* magazine. This instantly enhanced my credibility and literally had my phone ringing the very next day.

Even one piece of media coverage can make a huge difference to your practice, so the investment of time can pay off handsomely.

If you want to establish yourself as a media presence, you need to make yourself available to the media at their convenience and you need to have something interesting to say.

We will talk about how you can use press releases to get publicity for your practice in the section on Genius Marketing Tools in the next chapter.

4. WRITING ARTICLES

Another way of establishing your personal brand and your expertise is to write regular articles about your area of expertise.

Have these articles published in media which reaches your target market. Also make sure there is a way that people can follow up with and contact you.

As with speaking, you can create a core article that you tailor slightly to meet the needs of different audiences.

You can have different variations, such as a short article for local newsletters and a longer one for professional journals.

As I shared before, if you're not confident about your writing skills, you can hire a writer or editor to help you create the first article and you can then make tweaks each time you use it.

Writing a few short articles is often a great way to start building your own confidence in your writing skills.

You'll probably quickly discover that you are happy to tackle longer articles on more complex topics, or have them appear in publications which reach a much wider audience.

When you establish a reputation with your writing, you may even be invited to submit a regular column in a local newspaper or other publication.

> **GENIUS CPA**
> The Genius CPA uses as many ways as possible to establish their expertise and to reach as much of their target market as possible with their message.
>
> **INSIGHT**

In the chapter on online marketing, we will talk more about how publishing articles online can help build your reputation and drive traffic to your website.

5. WRITING A BOOK

When you get into the habit of writing a few articles or special reports, it's not too big a leap to then consider publishing your own book.

A book is really just a series of articles or special reports strung together.

When you have your own published book, your personal brand is taken to a whole new level. As soon as you are a published author, people see you in a different way. It becomes much easier for you to attract prospective clients who want to learn more about you and how you can help them.

Until recently, publishing a book involved a complex process requiring agents and publishers. But these days, print on demand technology allows anyone to have a real book published and selling in just a short time frame.

You can even employ a ghostwriter to collaborate with you and to create the content that will go out in your name.

I found that my book *Straight Talk About Small Business Success in New Jersey* was one of the most powerful tools in growing my practice. The fact that I was the author of a published book established me as an expert and helped me build my personal brand in other ways – for example by getting more invitations to speak and submit articles to respected publications.

The other day, I was meeting with some business clients of mine – two owners who founded and operate a very successful elder care company. Towards the end of the meeting, they thanked me for writing my book.

Not knowing what prompted my clients to make that remark, I replied, "Oh, you are welcome, did you find the information I shared in it helpful?"

They said yes, it had been helpful, but – more importantly – they said that had it not been for the book, they would have never found me, since they are located about an hour north of my office.

One of the owners had come across my book at a local Barnes & Noble bookstore, and that had led them to me. Since coming on board as clients they have paid my firm fees in excess of $34,000, not counting fees generated from their referrals. All this was possible due to the book.

6. CREATING A PRODUCT

Another option to consider for building your personal brand and your profits is to turn your expertise into a product that you can sell to a much wider audience.

For example, you could package your knowledge as an e-book or an audio program advising people on how to save on taxes. It could be something you sell for a relatively low price in order to reach a wide market.

This enables you to build your market beyond your local area and move from being a local firm to a national or global one.

Clearly many of the services you provide may require that you have personal contact with clients, but others can or could easily be delivered using alternative modes of communication.

There is thus the possibility that many of the people who buy your low-cost product will turn into longer-term clients.

Nevertheless, one of the advantages of offering your own product is that it builds your brand and allows you to add a new stream of revenue to your practice.

7. BLOGGING

Many Genius CPAs are now using blogging as a way to build their reputation and establish themselves as thought leaders in their respective fields, and in the process attract clients.

I will address blogging in more detail in the online marketing section; however, it is worth mentioning a couple of ways in which you can use blogging to build your personal brand.

Having your own blog – which can be connected to or separate from your practice website – allows you to talk about relevant issues and provide information that is helpful to your clients and prospective clients.

A blog is more than a website – it is a two-way communication tool. People can comment on your writing and can share your content through their social networks.

Another way to use blogging is to comment on other blogs that are seen by your target market and where your expertise can add value.

You can also arrange to publish guest posts on other people's blogs that reach the same audience in which you are interested.

8. NETWORKING

Networking may be one of the oldest and most popular forms of marketing but it's still one of the most effective ways of getting known and building your personal brand.

If you follow the right approach, networking can help you:

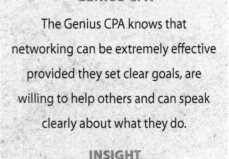

GENIUS CPA

The Genius CPA knows that networking can be extremely effective provided they set clear goals, are willing to help others and can speak clearly about what they do.

INSIGHT

- Build your contact list fast.

- Establish valuable business relationships.

- Get connected with the business community that you practice in.

But there is definitely an art to doing it effectively.

I have been networking since I started my practice fifteen years ago. These days, I am a little more selective about where I network and whom I network with. This has allowed me to put the effort in where it will achieve the best results.

When I started my practice, I joined several local chambers and also attended a weekly leads group. As time went on, I realized that some of these were not helping me develop the types of relationships that I wanted. This doesn't mean that they weren't useful groups; they just weren't the right ones for me.

But it's all very well to be told, "Get out there and network!"

**It's a fact that many practitioners just aren't
overly skilled at networking.**

Here are a few of the qualities that I have observed that make a practitioner a successful networker:

- **A genuine desire to help others.** Showing a commitment to building trust and truth in relationships will pay dividends.

- **Establishing definite goals for networking.** Making sure you have thought about what you want to achieve by networking will help you choose the right groups and get more out of them.

- **Willingness to volunteer.** Accepting volunteer positions in the groups you join helps you stay visible, and is a way of giving back to those who have helped you along your journey.

- **Good conversational skills.** Not everyone is a born conversationalist, but this is something that can be learned. Asking open-ended questions keeps the discussion going and can bring in all sorts of interesting points of view. It shows that you really are interested in what the other person has to say.

- **Listening skills.** The best advice I can give you is to listen more than you talk – after all, we've got two ears and only one mouth. Concentrate on what the other person is saying, listen to their tone of voice, and observe their body language.

- **A sense of timing.** People will be put off if you immediately launch into a sales pitch. Listen carefully and you'll know when to steer the conversation towards a business opportunity.

- **A resource for others.** If you are unfailingly helpful and knowledgeable, especially when it's obvious that there is no immediate benefit for you, people will remember you.

- **A clear understanding of what your firm does.** You need to be able to explain why you are better than other firms offering the same services, and you need to be able to do this in as few words as possible.

- **A clear understanding of what you want from others.** If someone offers to help you, you must be able to tell them what you need. People don't have the time or the energy to help you figure out what might be helpful for your firm.

- **Willingness to follow up.** If you are given a referral, act on it in a timely manner. People will quickly become tired of referring prospects to you if you don't act on them.

Think about the way you have been approaching your networking activities. If you are not making use of the suggestions above, now is the time to start improving your skills.

These are two great books I recommend for more tips on networking effectively:

- *Never Eat Alone: And Other Secrets to Success, One Relationship at a Time* by Keith Ferrazzi.

- *Networking for People Who Hate Networking: A Field Guide for Introverts, the Overwhelmed, and the Underconnected* by Devora Zack.

9. VIDEO MARKETING AND PODCASTING

I will delve more into video marketing in the section on online marketing, but this is another attractive way of building your personal brand.

In online marketing terms, one of the benefits of video marketing is that it drives traffic to your website.

However, for personal branding, video is a great way to establish your personality and your expertise.

The big advantage of video is that people can see you rather than simply read what you have to say. (Even if you don't appear on camera, they can still hear your voice in the audio.)

This creates a deeper relationship that makes them feel more comfortable about contacting you. In addition, the fact that you are using a medium that is still seen as relatively new establishes you as an expert in your prospect's eyes.

You can use video either on your own website or on sharing sites such as YouTube. You can create videos specifically to promote your practice and you can also use existing video, for example, from events where you have been speaking.

Podcasting is simply a way of publishing audio recordings to a wide audience through channels such as iTunes.

When you do this regularly, it is a little like having your own radio show. It appeals to many people, as recording a short audio is often much easier than writing an article or creating a video.

It is also a great way to share up-to-date information quickly and easily in a way that people find easy to consume.

CPAs who benefit most from podcasting tend to create and publish podcasts regularly rather than simply as occasional recordings.

10. SEMINARS AND WORKSHOPS

Speaking at seminars and workshops is a powerful way to establish your personal brand. Being an invited speaker at someone else's event automatically positions you as an expert.

In addition to speaking at other people's events, you can organize your own events and invite people to attend.

You can either use these for lead generation or they can be revenue generating on their own.

The secret of making presentations work is to find a topic that interests a large number of people and then give it an appealing title. Presentations can work particularly well at specific times of the year, such as the months leading to tax season for a topic on taxes.

To run an event of your own such as this, you will need to hire a hotel room or community hall and then promote the event by inviting people along.

You may get even better results by partnering with other complementary businesses that are interested in the same market.

11. TELESEMINARS AND WEBINARS

Teleseminars and webinars are a way of delivering the benefits of a live event without you or the audience having to leave home.

Teleseminars are run over the telephone – or through an internet connection – and usually last about an hour.

Webinars are similar, but involve people being able to see your presentation on their computer screen. This can be particularly useful if you have charts or information that works well visually.

As with live events, you can run your own or appear as a guest on somebody else's. They can be free and used primarily for lead generation or they can be paid events which generate revenue.

A major advantage of teleseminars and webinars is that they can be easily recorded and converted into products that you can sell or give away for lead generation purposes.

12. SOCIAL MEDIA

We go into the issue of social media in greater detail in the online marketing section. However it's important to mention that this is a valuable way of building your personal brand.

You can use your social networks to expand your reach and to promote your expertise.

Choose the top five or six tools you want to focus on and develop a plan to build your personal brand.

LEVERAGING EVERYTHING FOR MAXIMUM BENEFIT

Given the wide range of tools you can use to build and promote your personal brand, it may seem like a lot of work.

And it's true that you won't achieve a strong personal brand without a bit of hard work and effort. However the secret of making this work is to harness the power of leverage to make the same work deliver results for you over and over again.

There are two things I recommend that you establish in order to start building your personal brand.

- **Core Presentation:** This is the outline for a presentation that you can deliver on your chosen topic to virtually any audience.

- **Core Report:** This is a short report that you use to establish your expertise in your chosen area.

These two items will naturally be very closely linked. You will probably find that you develop one first and then create the other from it.

One easy way of creating your report is to deliver a presentation and have it recorded, and then use the transcription as the basis for creating your report. This works particularly well for people who are more confident about their ability to speak on a topic than to write about it.

Once you have these in place, the secret of building your personal brand quickly and efficiently is to leverage the same content over and over. For example, here are twelve ways you could leverage your core special report:

1. Offer it on your website as an incentive for people to join your email list.

2. Issue a press release highlighting the key points from the report and offering free copies to people who contact you.

3. Break the report into a series of short articles that you then publish online.

4. Use the content to create a series of blog posts on the topics you cover.

5. Develop a PowerPoint presentation from the content then add an audio and post on your website or on YouTube.

6. Record an audio of the content of the report and publish it as a podcast.

7. Use it as the outline of a script for teleseminar.

8. Create a one-page cheat sheet version of the report.

9. Turn the content into a longer article for local business magazines.

10. Blog about the report and share it on social media sites.

11. Send the report to event organizers as a hook to get invitations to speak at other groups and events.

12. Make it the first in a series which you can turn into a product to sell or use it as the first chapter in your book.

Of course you don't have to do all twelve and you certainly don't need to do them all at once.

This simply provides a series of activities that you can go through over time. The key is to always be thinking of new ways you can use the same work to make the most of what you put into it.

 **Identify at least five ways you can leverage a marketing piece you have already created.**

Personal and Practice Branding:
TOP MISTAKES TO AVOID

There are several mistakes that CPAs make when it comes to building a personal brand. Here are some of the most common:

- **Trying to be all things.** Most practicioners hesitate to specialize in one area because they are scared to close off other options. But you cannot be an expert on everything. The secret is to find an area that is broad enough to appeal to a wide range of people and which keeps open the opportunity to work with them to meet their other needs.

- **Waiting for permission.** Some CPAs are a little too shy or modest to position themselves as an expert. It's almost like they are waiting for someone to tell them it's okay. The truth is we get so close to our knowledge that we don't realize how much others value it. Take some time to think about what people ask you about most. Part of being an expert is keeping up to date but too many practitioners think they have one more thing they need to learn before they can establish their expertise.

- **Not focusing on the audience.** It's always tempting for us as professionals to get bogged down in the technical detail of what we do. However, to build a personal brand, we need to think about our clients and their problems and position what we do in response to their needs. People are interested in what we do for them and not how we do it.

- **Failing to leverage.** Many people waste time by repeating the same work over and over, and this can be exhausting. The secret to getting the best results in personal branding is by leveraging.

- **Trying to do too much.** The other side of failing to leverage is the risk of trying to do too much. You might look at the list of twelve ideas I covered and get overwhelmed, thinking there is no time to do them all. The fact is you don't have to do them all and you certainly don't have to do them all at once. Taking one step at a time is often the best way to success.

KEYS TO SUCCESS

- The three steps to creating an effective personal brand are:
  1. Identify your specific field of expertise.
  2. Choose the tools you want to use to promote your expertise.
  3. Leverage everything for maximum benefit.

- The best tools to build your personal brand include:
  - White papers and special reports
  - Public speaking
  - Writing articles
  - Writing a book
  - Creating a product
  - Blogging
  - Networking
  - Video marketing and podcasting
  - Seminars and workshops
  - Teleseminars and webinars
  - Press releases
  - Social marketing

- To leverage everything for maximum benefit create the following items and then adapt them in as many ways as possible for maximum impact.
  - Core presentation
  - Core report

Make a note of the additional key points from this chapter and what actions you are going to take as a result.

4

PROMOTION AND ADVERTISING:

Getting Your Practice's Message Across to Your Target Market

"If you don't believe in your product, or if you're not consistent and regular in the way you promote it, the odds of succeeding go way down."

JAY CONRAD LEVINSON
AUTHOR AND CREATOR OF *GUERRILLA MARKETING*

ONE REASON many CPA practitioners don't get the results they want from their marketing is that they don't know the difference between Genius marketing and poor marketing.

The truth is that most businesses practice poor marketing. The characteristics of poor marketing are as follows:

- Talks about the advertiser instead of the prospect.

- Is solely focused on building awareness of your name.

- Does not ask for a specific response from the reader.

- Has no means to measure its effectiveness.

- Does not differentiate the advertiser from the competition.

Poor marketing is usually a waste of money. Often, the problem is that the advertiser doesn't know the money is wasted because they have no way of checking.

It's surprising that, as a profession responsible in one way or another for our clients' money, we waste so much of our own money on poor advertising and marketing. We should concentrate on Genius marketing instead, which:

- Focuses on the prospect and their needs.

- Encourages the prospect to take specific action such as making a phone call or visiting a website, hence referred by top marketers as "direct response" marketing.

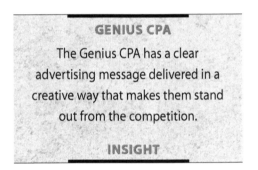

GENIUS CPA
The Genius CPA has a clear advertising message delivered in a creative way that makes them stand out from the competition.

INSIGHT

- Has specific results which can be tracked and measured.

- Stands out from the competition because of its distinctive message.

- Is targeted to a specific audience.

In this section we'll be looking at how to implement Genius marketing and advertising.

We will be covering it in the following two sections:

- **Genius marketing tools:** Different types of marketing and advertising you can use.

- **Genius marketing techniques:** How to use these tools to get the best results possible.

As I mentioned in the chapter on personal branding, you need to find a way to make you and your firm stand out from the competition.

One of the places where you really notice how all CPAs look the same is when you check out the "accountants" section in the Yellow Pages. You'll see that all the ads are very similar. Few, if any, stand out.

That's what Las Vegas EA Mary S. Fries of Tax Divas LLC noticed when she was planning to place an ad there.

Advertising had never worked for her previously, so she wondered if there was any point in trying it again. She had found her main source of new clients – referrals from other professionals – was not working as well due to the weak economy.

So she decided to look at other options, though she knew this time she'd need a different approach.

When she looked at the Yellow Pages, she noticed that all her competitors had half page ads with lots of small type, and none of them stood out.

Then she realized that her previous advertising had been just the same.

So this time she opted to be different and chose to run a color ad the size of a business card – where one third is her picture.

It simply states, "Tax Problems? Former IRS Officer," and gives her contact details.

It lists only three services – tax representation, tax preparation, and book-keeping. She has found that simple is definitely best.

She says: "People comment on being able to see who I am and that it's read-able – there is no tiny print. The ad highlights my greatest attribute – being a former IRS officer and this sets me apart from all the others."

Within a few days of the ad first appearing, it was already generating calls.

She adds: "People are remarking how simple and straightforward my ad appears to them."

The same principle applies to all types of advertising. You need to have a clear message that makes you stand out from the competition.

When you have no way of standing out from your competition, not many people will call you Even when people do call you, they'll ask how much you charge because they'll have no way of seeing you as different – apart from your fees.

When you use Genius marketing, you stand out from the rest and prospective clients are inclined to contact you. They know there is a reason to do business with you and don't put the focus on fees.

TWO-STEP MARKETING

Before we start to look at how to implement Genius marketing, there is one important concept to understand.

When you reach out to anyone, whether it is through advertising, direct mail, publicity, or any other channel, the odds are against you that they'll want your services right away.

A large chunk of the people who see your advertising are in the category that we would call "interested but not ready."

There are prospects who may well have a need for your services, but either the present moment is not right or they are not yet convinced. In poor marketing, you would lose most of these people as they are not yet ready to purchase your services.

With Genius marketing, you establish a means to keep in touch with these folks so that you build a relationship. This means you are in touch with them when the moment is right for them to consider your services.

We call this two-step marketing because the first step involves having them give you their contact details so that you can send them some information, such as a free report.

The second step involves keeping in regular touch with them so that you have a pool of prospects who will be ready to contact you when they need your services.

This process is also known as lead generation, as you are using it to build a list of people or leads that could turn into future clients. We will discuss how to keep in touch with this group of prospects in the chapter on relationship building.

GENIUS MARKETING TOOLS

In this section, I'll focus on the steps you can take to build the list of leads. This process also carries through into the section on online marketing in Chapter 5.

Genius marketing tools include the following four categories:

- Advertising
- Direct mail and postcards
- Press releases
- Other offline tools

ADVERTISING

There are several different types of advertising that we will discuss. However, the most important point to remember is that your advertising should always be focused on getting people to take a specific action.

In some cases that will be to call your office directly in response to a particular offer. However, it will often be to request information, such as a free report, that you use as an incentive for them to give you their contact details.

The different types of advertising you might consider are as follows:

- **Display Advertising:** These are the large ads that appear in newspapers and magazines. Display advertising may be appropriate if you have a highly targeted publication, are offered a very attractive price to advertise, or you use the "advertorial" approach. Advertorials are ads which appear in the same style as the editorial copy of the publication. Even though people know they are advertisements, they tend to attract more interest and response. Any advertising you do should adhere to the Genius marketing criteria I shared at the beginning of this chapter.

- **Classified Advertising:** Some professional practices turn up their noses at using classified advertising. However, many people look through classified advertising sections of local and specialist newspapers for listings of service providers that they need.

  As classified advertising can be quite inexpensive, it's also a very effective way to generate leads by offering a special report and inviting people to call a hotline or visit your website to request it.

- **Yellow Pages:** Until recently, the Yellow Pages was one of the most important places to advertise. It was the place where virtually everybody went to look for a service provider.

  Nowadays, it is declining in importance and people are much more likely to use online methods and local search – we talk about that in more detail in the online marketing section.

  Nevertheless, the Yellow Pages remains an important place for CPAs to have an effective presence. As I explained with the example of Mary Fries, having the right ad can give you great results. I continue to use the Yellow Pages to promote my practice because the return I get from the media is a multiple of my investment in it.

- **TV and Radio:** Many practice owners would see TV and radio as being beyond their reach. However, in some situations, it can be a very cost-effective way to reach your target market. This applies if you can find a channel that delivers the exact type of client you're looking for. It can also work if you are able to use the low-cost options such as late-night advertising or online radio. Again, TV and radio advertising should always be two-step marketing focused on encouraging people to take a specific action.

DIRECT MAIL AND POSTCARDS

Following the right direct mail strategies can be a very cost-effective way of building your client base.

The key to getting the best out of direct mail is being able to reach the exact market you want with an effective message.

One of the big advantages of direct mail is that it allows you to accurately track and measure the results you get.

Success depends on having a good mailing list. You may be able to get lists of target clients through links with a local trade association or Chamber of Commerce or you could purchase lists from providers such as InfoUSA.com.

Direct mail can be as simple as sending out a letter or it can involve a more sophisticated information packet. Refer to the section later on in this chapter titled "lumpy mail."

Other variations of direct mail include:

- **Postcards:** These can be very effective, as they are cheap and easy to produce. They are especially useful for:
  - o Generating leads by encouraging people to request a free report.
  - o Staying in touch with long-term prospects.
  - o Running a sequence to promote something specific.

- **Tearsheets:** These are news articles printed on newspaper to look as though they are genuine newspaper articles. These will often arrive in the post with a sticky post-it note attached seeming to be a personal message. However, the content of these articles is actually an advertising message.

- **Valpaks and Card Decks:** You can also get the benefits of direct response using card decks and Valpaks. These are small card sets or booklets mailed to a targeted audience. This can work well if it reaches the exact target market you're looking for – as the production and mailing costs are shared by a number of advertisers. You can use these as another way to encourage people to give you their contact details.

PRESS RELEASES

As I mentioned in Chapter 3, publicity is one of the best ways to establish a reputation as an expert and attract new prospective clients.

People tend to believe things much more when they read them in the editorial columns rather than appearing as an advertisment. Therefore if you can be reported or quoted positively in the media, this helps build your reputation.

One of the keys to getting publicity is sending out press releases. The best thing about a press release is that it is free and, if the media chooses to run with your story, it gives you easy access to a multitude of new prospective clients that you might otherwise not be able to "touch."

Personally, I've had great success with press releases; my articles have appeared in various publications throughout the country, including *Accounting Today, The CPA Journal, Chiropractic Economics, Two River Times, Financial Advisor* and *Wealth Manager.*

The media is constantly looking for information they can share with their readers so, if you have something interesting to say, you should let them know. However, a press release has to be different from an advertising message. It has to deliver information that editors believe would interest their readers.

Creating a Press Release

One reason many practitioners hesitate to send out press releases is that they are not sure what makes for an appropriate topic. Here are some examples of topics that might make an effective press release:

- **Solution to a problem:** Issue a release giving the solution to a problem shared by many people – such as completing your tax returns on time or how to avoid IRS audits.

- **Tips and advice:** Position yourself as an expert by providing advice on your area of expertise, e.g., "10 Ways to Save On Taxes." This type of release is not tied to a particular date and can be used at any time by the media.

- **Comments on the news:** If you have relevant views on something in the news – such as the impact on small businesses of new tax proposals – issue a release giving your comments.

- **Publish a report:** When you publish a report or white paper, send it to the media with a press release summarizing the key points and telling readers how they can get a copy.

- **Host an event:** Any event – ranging from an office opening to a seminar – is a reason to issue a press release and an opportunity to invite the media along.

- **Launch something new:** Whenever you make a major change in your firm – such as launching a new service – this is of interest to the media.

Putting together a press release does not have to be complicated. The most important elements that it should include are:

- Strong headline to attract interest.

- Brief summary of the key message.

- Opening paragraph summarizing the key points and drawing readers in.

- Body content providing the key information and any quotes.

- Conclusion summarizing the release and explaining how to get further information.

Your release should include your direct contact information and you need to make yourself available so that the media can get in touch for more details.

Issuing Your Press Release

Once you have your press release, the next step is to issue it to the relevant media. The exact people you send it to will depend on whether the story is of local, industry or national importance.

As we'll discuss in the next chapter, there are also various online resources you can use to distribute your press release. One of the most popular is PRWeb.com, which provides some great tips and advice on how to create effective press releases.

However, while online resources and emails are now extremely important, it is also prudent to send hard copies and follow up with telephone calls.

Press releases offer no guarantee of instant success but, when your first articles appear in print, you'll wonder why you haven't used this approach before.

And when you get a great result, you'll realize it's one of the best ways of promoting your practice and building awareness of your expertise.

> For more publicity tips, download a free recording of my interview with publicity expert Joan Stewart titled: *"How to Promote Your CPA Practice Using Online and Offline Publicity Tools and Strategies"* as part of the Reader-Only Special Bonus at www.TheUltimateCPAPractice.com/free.html

OTHER OFFLINE TOOLS

There are many more offline advertising and marketing tools you can use to attract more clients. Here are some examples:

- **Voice and fax broadcasts:** These are standard messages sent to a list of phone or fax numbers. You simply write or record the message and the rest is done automatically. The "Do Not Call" rules will limit how much you can use these.

- **Trade shows and events:** These can be an appropriate way to meet people in your market whether you just attend or take a stand.

- **Creative business cards:** One way of standing out is to have a business card that is more distinctive than others – perhaps because of its odd shape or size. Another effective way to make the best use of business cards is to have a message on the back – which may be an invitation to visit your website for your free report.

- **Charity involvement and sponsorship:** This can be an attractive way to build new contacts and to establish a position in your community. It also has networking benefits because of the connections you will make.

Identify which offline marketing tools you are going to use to promote your practice.

GENIUS MARKETING TECHNIQUES

Now that we have covered the tools of Genius marketing, we'll look at some of the techniques you can use to get the best results. The three we'll look at are:

- The Art of Writing Copy

- The Power of Creativity

- Testing and Tracking

THE ART OF WRITING COPY

One of the most important skills for attracting new clients and building relationships is the ability to communicate your offer persuasively.

When practitioners hear that top copywriters charge thousands of dollars for creating just a few pages of copy, they become discouraged and end up not even trying to write their own sales letters and marketing material.

However, the truth is that writing copy to create advertising and sales letters – both online and offline – is much easier than you might think.

Even the top copywriters often use a template or follow a standard formula to create their letters. You know your practice and what you offer better than anyone else and have more passion attached to it. There is thus no reason that you can't follow the same formula in order to create a winning sales letter or advertisement.

The exact approach you follow will depend on what type of item you are creating as crafting a postcard is clearly very different from writing a long sales letter. However, many of the principles apply to all types of persuasive communication.

In the chapter on positioning, I talked about the importance of having a clear picture of your ideal client. It's important that you hold this picture in your mind in any sales communication.

You will always be more natural and persuasive if you imagine yourself communicating with one person rather than an anonymous group.

When you have your audience in mind, this is the 12-step process you should follow to create effective marketing.

1. Headline: Get Their Attention

The most important part of any communication – whether it is a sales letter, advertisement, blog post or article – is the headline.

The headline is your chance to capture people's attention and tell them you have something interesting to say. The entire purpose of the headline is to make people stop and read more.

Many top copywriters will spend a large percentage of their time on the headline and come up with many different options before choosing the right one. It is therefore worth spending time working on your headline to make sure it captures the attention of your prospects.

Headline Formula Examples

Make a Promise
"I'll Show You 10 Ways To Save $10,000 On Your Tax Bill"

 # Reasons
"Six Reasons You're Paying The Government Too Much In Tax"

Discover
"Discover How You Can Save $10,000 On Your Tax Bill Today"

If... Then...
"If Your Tax Records Are In A Mess Then You Need This Free Tool"

Curiosity
"How One Small Business Saved $10,000 In Tax Last Year"

There are a number of formulas you can follow to come up with a good headline. Some examples are shown in the box.

You can enhance the power of the headline by introducing two other elements:

- **Pre-headline:** This is a short sentence that appears before the headline and can be used to highlight for whom the message is best suited. For example: "Attention Small Business Owners."

- **Post-headline:** This is a short sentence that appears after the headline and is useful to build on the message from the headline or to be more specific. For example: "Free Report Shows How You Can Cut Your Tax Bill Starting Today."

2. Problem: Identify With What They Want

If you want to sell something, you have to show the reader that you have a solution to their problem. Your letter needs to reiterate the problem and encourage them to take action to solve it. Copywriters call this "agitating the problem."

Somebody reading your letter should be thinking "Yeah, that's exactly how I feel. I want to do something about it."

3. Solution: Tell Them How You Can Help

Now that you have reminded them about the problem, the next step is to introduce yourself as the solution. At this stage, you are not going into great detail. You simply want to let them know there is a ready solution to the problem and that they just need to keep reading to find out what it is.

4. Credentials: Explain Why You Are Best Placed to Help

So far, you have caught their attention and talked about *them* and *their* problem. Now you need to establish your credentials and demonstrate why you are the right person to help them. You need to tell them about your relevant experience and expertise that positions you and your practice as being able to help them better than anyone else.

5. Benefits: Demonstrate How Your Solution Will Help

The next stage in the process is to highlight the benefits to them of taking the action you suggest. This is where many CPA practitioners make the mistake of going into detail about systems and processes, rather than concentrating on what this means for the client.

It is very important to understand the difference between features and benefits:

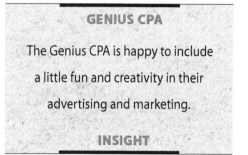

GENIUS CPA

The Genius CPA is happy to include a little fun and creativity in their advertising and marketing.

INSIGHT

- **Features** are the facts and the characteristics of a product or service.

- **Benefits** are what this means to the person.

For example, if you offer fixed fees, that is a feature of your service. The benefit of this is that there are no unpleasant surprises for the client when they receive your bill. If you work to a specific timetable, that is a feature but the benefit to the client is that they are guaranteed never to pay any late-fee penalties.

Your aim is to identify as many benefits as possible of your product or service. Usually the best way to communicate benefits is to list them in the form of short bullet points that focus on what advantages they deliver to the client.

6. Social Proof: Show How It Has Helped Others

Marketing material and sales letters cover how great you are and talk positively about the solutions you offer. However, people are naturally suspicious and skeptical so they like to know that somebody else has had good results from something before they are willing to give it a try. This is called "social proof."

Powerful testimonials from clients telling their success stories will help prospects see how they can benefit from working with you. This also allows your clients to talk about the benefits of your services.

Testimonials should always be genuine and based on typical results. In some States, there may be restrictions about what information you can use in testimonials.

In the chapter on partnership with clients, we will talk more about testimonials and how to get them.

7. Offer: Explain In More Detail What You Will Do

The next part of your letter is where you start going into detail to explain your precise offer and what you will deliver. For example, you could provide a description of what is included in the service you are promoting.

8. Guarantee: Remove the Risk from their Decision

No matter how effective your sales letter, there will be many people who are genuinely interested but are hesitating about their decision to move forward. You can take away all the risk involved in their decision by offering some sort of guarantee.

The exact guarantee you offer will depend on the product or service for example you may offer people money back if they are not satisfied or else guarantee a specific outcome. Guarantees give people greater comfort when making their choice and demonstrate your confidence in your services.

9. Scarcity: Give Them a Reason to Act Now

Even though you may have done a great job with your sales letter, people always have other priorities and demands on their time and they may be tempted to hesitate before making a purchase decision. They may be planning to wait until the end of the month or plan to come back tomorrow.

However, the reality is that they normally won't come back after they have read your letter. So you need to find a way to make them take action today. You can do this by including scarcity in your offer. For example, this could be in the form of having limited spots available or a deadline for a special offer.

Scarcity should always be used with integrity. If you say you only have 25 places available, or that there is a time limit on the price, make sure you follow these. If you don't, sooner or later it will be discovered and it will damage your reputation.

10. Call to Action: Tell Them Exactly What to Do

A surprising mistake that many practitioners make with sales letters is that they don't tell the reader exactly what they should do. You must tell them what the next step is, whether to call your office, visit your website or make a purchase. You need to make this process as clear and simple as possible.

11. Warning: Highlight the Consequences of Not Acting

As you move towards the end of the letter, you need to highlight any consequences of not taking action. Remind them about the problem and how the problem will continue if they don't do something about it today.

12. P.S.: Remind Them of the Benefits

Research shows that the PS at the end is often the most widely read part of a sales letter. So your letter should normally include at least one PS. It is an opportunity to re-emphasize the benefits and encourage them to take action now.

 **Write a sales letter for your main product or service.**

THE POWER OF CREATIVITY

You can get better results from your marketing and advertising by stepping outside the traditional approaches.

Many CPAs assume that because they are in a professional business, this means they have to be "formal" in their marketing communication. Nothing could be further from the truth.

The cardinal mistake I see most practitioners make when I review the marketing materials they've sent to me for critique is that their ads and sales letters are dry and boring.

Your prospective clients want a little bit of excitement in their lives, so anything you can do to make your marketing more fun and interesting will attract their attention.

Here are some ways to do this:

- **Lumpy Mail:** If you're sending out a direct mail piece, include something on it or in it that makes them more likely to take notice.

  For example you could have an aspirin on the front of your envelope or postcard with a message saying: *"Is Your Tax Bill Giving You A Massive Headache?"*

  Or you could include something in the envelope that makes it "lumpy." It could be a pen or it could be a baseball bat but anything that makes your package stand out as different from the rest in their mailbox makes it more likely to get their attention.

  You want to make sure your mail goes into the pile they will read now and not the pile they say they will read later but never get around to, or worse, mail that goes directly into their trash can, unopened and unread.

- **Office Redesign:** Another way of being creative is to make the experience of coming to your office one that is more attractive for your clients. You could do this by the way it is painted, by the furnishing you choose or by setting up a coffee shop. There are many ways to make the experience of working with you more fun and more pleasant for your clients.

- **New places to advertise:** You can also be creative in the places you advertise. This may be through advertising in non-business publications or it may be by hanging a banner in an unusual location. A little creativity may enable you to get great results while paying less money.

 **Identify some creative ways to promote your practice.**

TESTING AND TRACKING

A crucial part of getting the best results from your marketing is making sure that you track and test everything. You want to find out the impact of different headlines, different marketing techniques and different offers in order to keep improving the results.

That's one of the reasons why it's important to have a direct response approach to marketing rather than one simply focused on getting better known.

Direct response ensures that you have some way of accurately measuring the results of your marketing activity – whether it is in the number of leads you generate or the value of new clients you attract.

 **Define how you are going to track your advertising and marketing results.**

Promotion and Advertising:
TOP MISTAKES TO AVOID

Here are common mistakes that CPAs make in their advertising and marketing activity:

- **Relying on one-step marketing.** Most prospects who see your marketing will not be ready to engage your firm right away. However your marketing may not be in front of them when they are ready. You therefore need to take the opportunity to collect their contact details so that you can keep in touch with them.

- **Running brand-building advertising.** Marketing that is simply designed to make people aware of your practice is a waste of your money. You should spend your budget on advertising that is designed to create a specific response such as contacting you for information.

- **Being too boring.** While we are in a professional business, everybody likes a little fun in their day. You can therefore attract more attention and stand out by being more creative in the way you get your message across.

- **Missing out on opportunities for publicity.** Publicity is a great way to get your firm known without spending a great deal of money. Many CPAs are too shy in sharing their message because they are under the misconception that they have nothing interesting to say.

- **Not creating a plan.** When you create a calendar or plan of your marketing activities, it is much easier to coordinate to ensure you make the best use of your time and budget. When you don't have a plan, you often end up not taking action in times when you're busy and then don't have a steady flow of new prospects when things are quieter.

KEYS TO SUCCESS

- Advertising
    - Display Advertising
    - Classified Advertising
    - Yellow Pages
    - TV and Radio

- Direct Mail
    - Postcards
    - Tearsheets
    - Card Decks and Valpaks

- Press Releases

- The Art of Writing Copy
    1. Heading
    2. Problem
    3. Solution
    4. Credentials
    5. Benefits
    6. Social Proof
    7. Offer
    8. Guarantee
    9. Scarcity
    10. Call to Action
    11. Warning
    12. P.S.

Make a note of the additional key points from this chapter and what actions you are going to take as a result.

5

POWERFUL ONLINE PRESENCE:

Using the Internet Effectively to Reach More People and Build Your Brand

----

*"The more informative your advertising,
the more persuasive it will be."*

DAVID OGILVY
ADVERTISING EXECUTIVE, 1911 - 1999

THESE DAYS virtually no business or professional practice can ignore the important role that the internet plays in promoting its services, attracting clients, and building your personal brand.

Many fail to make the most of it because they are intimidated and overwhelmed by the technology, the pace of change, and the range of options available.

If you take time to develop a plan and to work out the most important actions to take in your own situation, online marketing can offer huge potential.

In this chapter, we'll look at the key priorities you should set and the actions you need to take to reap the full benefits of online marketing. We cover the following steps:

- Creating your online home with a website or blog.

- Driving traffic to your website to attract as many of your ideal visitors as possible.

- Strategies for turning your website visitors into long-term clients.

- Building your presence beyond your website using social media.

- Tracking and analytics to monitor and assess the efficacy of your actions.

Taking action in each of these areas will enable you to make the internet an important source of business for your practice.

CREATING YOUR ONLINE HOME

A large proportion of people now go online when they're looking for information about almost anything.

If somebody is looking for a CPA in your area or they have heard of you and want to know more about you, they will almost inevitably go and do an online search or look for your website.

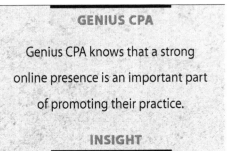

If you don't have an established web presence, you are effectively saying that you don't exist for a large chunk of your prospective market.

A few years ago, many practitioners got burned because they spent a fortune on website design and discovered it did not produce satisfactory results. However, nowadays there is no need to spend huge sums to establish a professional presence.

When I started getting involved online about ten years ago, there were lots of CPAs with websites. However the problem was that they were all canned websites and looked very similar to each other. They were really just like corporate brochures and none of them stood out.

Yet the truth is that the majority of professional practices' websites that I come across still fall into that category today. They all look the same and they don't connect with what prospective clients are looking for.

I found I got much better results from my website when I started to make use of direct response ideas online.

The key to direct response methods is that they are focused on getting people to take specific actions, such as asking for more information.

I also got a much better response by being more personal and establishing a connection with the visitor. You want the person visiting your site to be able to relate to you and your team.

That's why it's so important that your website reflect your personality as the practice owner, and that of your team, as well as the identity of your practice on the whole.

On my site, we have photos of the team plus comments from them. It helps to build a relationship with clients and prospects.

You want people to visit your site and think, "These guys understand my problems."

FIVE KEYS TO CREATING AN EFFECTIVE WEBSITE

Here are five factors you should take into account to establish an effective website:

1. Establish a Clear Purpose

As with any aspect of your practice, you need to be able to evaluate the success of your website. However, you can only do this if you have a clear sense of purpose.

The single most important reason for having a website, besides conveying your identity and brand, is to help build new relationships and deepen existing ones. In other words, it is to encourage folks who are interested in your services to get in touch with you.

The way you do that is by giving them a prominent invitation to share with you their contact information. In order to do that, you will need to offer some sort of incentive, such as a white paper, free report or downloadable audio. We will cover this in greater detail in Chapter 6.

2. Keep It Simple

There is no need to make your website complicated. In many situations, the simpler the better.

Here are the key pages you must have on your website.

- **Home Page:** The main purpose of the home page is to encourage people to give you their contact information so it needs to be compelling enough to attract their attention and connect with you.

- **About Us:** The majority of folks that visit your site do so because they are interested in finding out more about you so explain a little bit about your practice and the people that work there.

- **Services:** You need to provide details of the services you offer but convey the descriptions from a client perspective.

- **Contact Us:** You should make it as easy as possible for the visitor to contact you using the method of their choice, including email address, physical address, phone number, and fax number.

- **Clients and Testimonials:** Prospects who are interested in becoming your client want to know a little about the clients you already have, so one of the most important parts of your website is providing testimonials from other satisfied clients.

If your website adequately covers these five elements, you are better placed than most of your competitors. It is much better to keep the site simple and clean rather than bog it down with too much detail or distracting flash animation.

GENIUS CPA

The Genius CPA knows that the keys to an effective website are first catching the visitor's attention and then giving them a reason to share their contact details.

INSIGHT

Nevertheless there are additional sections and pages you can add to your site if you wish. For example, you may want to include a number of articles relevant to your audience. You may also want to provide free resources that would be useful to them.

3. Grab Their Attention

When someone visits your site, you only have a few seconds in which to captivate their interest. You need to show them quickly why they should take an interest in you and the services you offer.

The most important way to attract the attention of website visitors is to have a strong benefit-oriented headline at the top of your page. Many practices and businesses waste this space by having their logo or irrelevant graphics.

An effective web page will follow the key elements of the Art of Writing Copy that we covered in the previous chapter.

Your website does not have to sell your services to your prospective clients. Your main priority is to get them to give you their contact details so that you can stay in touch and to provide compelling reasons to contact you for an initial meeting.

4. Keep Asking for Their Contact Information

The biggest mistake that many website owners make is that they don't ask for the visitors' contact information. Make this a priority.

However, even those that do ask for contact details don't do so often enough.

You must make sure that the invitation to sign up to your email list is prominent and easy to understand. People need to be told exactly what to do. That means you need to give them very simple instructions such as "Enter your email address here."

The opt-in box should be on every page and perhaps several times on the most important pages.

5. Make Sure the Site is Visitor Friendly

Your website should be visually appealing and look professional. That means using clear typefaces with lots of white space.

You should include illustrations or photographs to be easy on the eye – use large text and different colors to highlight important information. However, going too far with too many different colors and typeface variations is distracting and puts visitors off.

Avoid distracting gimmicks, especially where they might make the webpage load slowly or not even work in some people's web browsers.

Even though your site may only have a few pages, it should be easy for people to identify where to find the information they need. This means you need to provide clear navigation along the top or at the side that makes it easy for them to find what they're looking for.

Good use of headlines and sub-headlines makes it easy for them to scan and decide what action to take. It also helps if your content is easy to read and broken up into small sections.

BLOGGING FOR SUCCESS

The growing popularity of blogging in recent years has meant that many practices have seen the value of creating a blog alongside or in place of their website.

A blog makes it easy to add new content regularly.

The advantages of using a blog include:

- Building your credibility by posting relevant content about your market regularly.

- Creating a hub for your social media network by allowing these posts to be shared through Facebook, Twitter and other similar sites.

- Attracting additional traffic and subscribers when these posts are shared.

- Enhancing your credibility as the regular posts build up into a valuable resource of articles and information.

- Improving your search engine ranking as a result of the regular posting of new information.

Blogs can be created easily using technology hosted on other sites such as Blogger.com and TypePad.com.

Many people are attracted to the benefits of hosting the blog on their own site using WordPress software (wordpress.org). Having the blog hosted on your website helps attract more traffic and gives you more flexibility in terms of the presentation and branding.

WordPress now offers a great deal of design flexibility and many people find that using this approach means they no longer need a separate conventional website.

Reasons to Blog

When you have a blog, you can use it for several purposes, including:

- Commenting on news and issues relevant to your clients.

- Providing educational and background information to help your clients.

- Sharing information about what's happening in your practice to strengthen relationships with clients.

- Having external experts provide relevant content that is helpful to your clients.

- Allowing two-way communication with clients and prospects to build relationships.

Keys to making sure your post is interesting

- Creating a strong headline that grabs the reader's attention.

- Providing useful, funny or controversial content.

- Presenting content in the format of bullets or lists.

- Featuring keywords that people are searching for.

- Appealing illustrations or graphics that attract attention.

- Holding competitions and conducting polls or surveys.

Review your website and make a plan for any changes needed, including deciding whether to have a blog alongside or instead of your website.

SEVEN STRATEGIES FOR DRIVING TRAFFIC TO YOUR WEBSITE

Regardless of how great your website is, it does not achieve its objectives unless you attract a lot of visitors.

In this section we look at seven different ways you can generate traffic to your website. These are:

1. Search Engine Optimization

2. Local Search

3. Online Advertising

4. Articles

5. Press Releases

6. Video Marketing

7. Offline Activity

Not all of these will be appropriate for every practice and it's generally best not to try and do everything at once. The secret is to decide what is best for you and concentrate on getting one strategy right before moving on to the next.

However, in the long term, you should never rely on just one source of traffic. Always be looking to have traffic coming in as many ways as possible

Why? So that if one underperforms, you have the others continuing to bring in a steady stream of new visitors.

1. SEARCH ENGINE OPTIMIZATION

When someone in your area goes online to look for information about services your CPA firm offers, you want to ensure that your practice website comes out among the top few in their search.

There are various steps you need to put in place to make sure your site ranks well and, if you do this, you have access to a great source of free targeted traffic. The process of ensuring that your website ranks well in the search engines is known as search engine optimization (SEO).

There are three key steps you can take to improve your search engine ranking.

1. **Choose the right keywords.** When somebody is looking for information about a topic online, the word or phrase they enter into the search box is called the "keyword," and this is very important in your marketing.

   You need to identify the top keywords people use when searching for a CPA practice such as "CPA in Baltimore" or "How to save taxes." The more specific the keywords are the better, and longer phrases are usually more effective.

   You can find popular keywords using the Google AdWords Keyword Tool (see the Resources section at the end of this chapter for details).

2. **Optimize Your Pages:** Once you have identified your top keywords, you need to make sure they appear regularly on your pages. Each page on your site is ranked separately so you need to repeat the process for each page. You may want each page to rank for different keywords.

   Your webmaster can ensure that the background coding of your website pages is structured properly to satisfy the search engines. Two key areas to look out for are the "meta title" which describes your page contents and the "meta page description" which is the short paragraph that will appear under the title in a Google search.

3. **Build Powerful Backlinks.** As well as the contents of your pages, search engines take into account "backlinks" from other sites. This is where an image, some text or your website URL appears on another website and is linked back to yours.

These backlinks are like votes for your site but each vote is not counted equally as Google gives a higher weighting to links from sites it sees as important. You can get high-quality links by publishing articles, posting videos, publishing press releases and appearing in trusted directories. We will cover some of these in more detail shortly.

2. LOCAL SEARCH

Recently Google and other search engines have been making significant changes which have increased the importance of Local Search.

Local Search is the maps and listings that show up when people are looking for a local service provider. Google knows that people value local search information and is giving it greater priority when delivering search results.

Your ranking in Local Search has nothing to do with your website and you need to take additional steps to ensure that your practice ranks well in Local Search.

In order to do this, you need to provide information to Google and make sure that the information in your online profiles is up to date.

There are additional steps you need to take, such as ensuring your practice is listed in important local directories and it also helps if you have listings in review sites.

When Superstar member Amanda Fisher of Barrington Business Professionals in New South Wales, Australia was asking clients for testimonials to use on her website, she also encouraged them to put reviews on Google, True Local or Merchant Circle.

She says: "I am currently the only accountant in my area with reviews on Google and have already received leads as a direct result."

She points out that these reviews and testimonials are also a great morale boost – particularly when you get glowing comments from a client that you weren't sure you had a great relationship with.

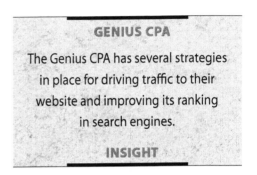

GENIUS CPA

The Genius CPA has several strategies in place for driving traffic to their website and improving its ranking in search engines.

INSIGHT

Local Search is certain to grow in importance as a way of finding and researching businesses of all types. As Amanda's experience shows, it doesn't take too much effort to be ahead of the curve but the rewards can be substantial.

People are already using Google Maps and Google Places – as well as the equivalents from Yahoo, Bing and other search engines – as a way of finding businesses.

3. ADVERTISING ONLINE

The fastest and easiest way to generate traffic to your website is through online advertising.

The most common type of online advertising is pay-per-click (PPC). These are the short ads that appear on search engine result pages, usually at the top and to the right of the page.

There are many advantages to PPC advertising, including:

- You only pay for people who click through on your ads.

- Campaigns can be started very quickly driving traffic to your site right away.

- Your ad is seen by people who are searching on your topic.

- You can easily track the effectiveness of your campaign.

- You can test different approaches easily to find out what works best.

The key elements of a PPC campaign are:

- **Keywords:** Which specific keywords you want to target. For example, if you bid on the term "Las Vegas CPA," your ad has a chance of appearing every time someone enters that search term.

- **Budget:** How much you can pay overall and for each click. The price of each keyword depends on the demand and can range from one cent for low usage keywords to several dollars for the most popular.

- **Copy:** The text of your ad.

The overall amount you are willing to pay for each click will depend on how successful you are at converting clicks into clients. You will only find this out over time through testing and by following up with people who contact you.

The level of your success in conversion is a combination of the copy in your ad – this will determine how many people click – and the process you have in place for following up with people.

While PPC has many attractions, it can also be very expensive if you don't follow the right strategy. So it's important to plan your campaign carefully and to track the results constantly.

While Google AdWords is the largest PPC provider, the other search engines offer similar services. In addition, advertising on Facebook and LinkedIn is becoming more popular and may provide a good way to reach highly targeted clients.

4. ONLINE ARTICLES

Writing articles for online publication is a great way to build your reputation and drive traffic to your website.

The best articles are fairly short – around 300 to 500 words works best – though they can occasionally be longer if you have particularly important content. You should keep each article focused on a single topic, ideally based around a relevant keyword.

After you have written your article, one of the easiest ways to get it published is by submitting it to an article directory or submission site. They will then publish your articles and syndicate them to other websites, publishers and directories.

Online articles benefit you when people read them and are intrigued. They click on a link at the end of the article and will be taken to your site, thus generating targeted traffic direct to your website.

Another advantage is that many article sites are ranked highly by Google and other search engines. The links from these articles back to your site can therefore count as quality backlinks to improve your search engine ranking.

Here are some of the best-known article sites:

www.ezinearticles.com

www.articlesbase.com

www.buzzle.com

When you write good content, choose good keywords and publish on quality sites. Writing articles can be a useful online marketing tactic.

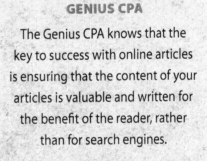

GENIUS CPA

The Genius CPA knows that the key to success with online articles is ensuring that the content of your articles is valuable and written for the benefit of the reader, rather than for search engines.

INSIGHT

5. ONLINE PRESS RELEASES

Online press releases are another terrific way to generate publicity and backlinks to your website.

As I have already highlighted in previous chapters, it's worthwhile to get in the habit of publishing press releases when you have something useful to say. This is a powerful way to promote your practice and build your personal brand.

In the chapters on personal branding and promotion, we talked about the value of publicity in building your personal brand and promoting your practice. Using online press releases gives you many of the same benefits and makes the process very easy. Often with a few tweaks you can even repurpose your articles to convert them into press releases.

The process of submitting your press release is similar to publishing an article.

However, when it comes to press releases, there are thousands of news sites, newsrooms, and trade magazines that will pick up your press release information and post it on their sites. They may even contact you for follow-up information so that they can write a more detailed article.

There are many free press release distribution services – which you can find through a Google search – but one of the top services is PRWeb.com.

6. VIDEO MARKETING

The idea of publishing video online may seem like something that is only open to firms with large budgets or specialist teams. However, these days, creating and uploading video is relatively easy.

A high proportion of online search is now driven by video and therefore publishing your own videos can help build your reputation and improve your search engine ranking.

You can easily create live video with equipment as simple as a $100 Flip-cam, though you may want to use more professional equipment in some circumstances, such as if you are being filmed speaking at a seminar.

Many high-quality videos are simply PowerPoint presentations with an audio soundtrack.

Whichever approach you choose, some of the best videos are only a minute or two long, so they don't need to be time-consuming to create.

The big advantage of video is that people get to experience more of you than they would by just reading your articles.

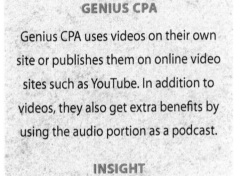

GENIUS CPA

Genius CPA uses videos on their own site or publishes them on online video sites such as YouTube. In addition to videos, they also get extra benefits by using the audio portion as a podcast.

INSIGHT

7. OFFLINE ACTIVITY

We covered the scope of offline marketing in more detail in the chapter on promotion and advertising, but it's important to remember that online activity and offline activity need to be integrated and work well together.

Naturally you want to include your web addresses in all your offline marketing. However many offline marketing activities often have the direct aim of driving people towards your website so you can collect their contact details.

Develop a strategy for driving traffic to your website.

TURNING VISITORS INTO CLIENTS

When someone visits your website, you want to make every effort to collect their contact information so that you can keep in touch with them.

In order to get them to share their information with you, you will need to offer them something of value as an incentive to do so. Examples of this include:

- Free report or a white paper.

- Free audio or video.

- Free resources such as checklists.

Whatever you offer needs to be relevant to your practice and perceived as valuable by your prospects. This can be promoted everywhere you invite people to sign up.

However, one of the biggest mistakes CPAs make with email marketing is that they collect the visitor's contact information and then fail to follow up with them.

These are people who have expressed interest in your practice and what you offer so they will lose interest if you don't contact them immediately. You also need to have a plan in place to follow up with them regularly.

Email is an ideal method for building relationships with your visitors. Some CPAs don't like to send out emails because they don't want to be seen as selling too hard. However, if someone has signed up to your list, they have raised their hand to express interest in what you're offering. They want to hear what you have to say.

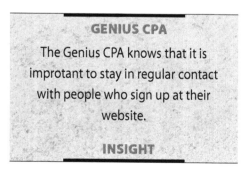

GENIUS CPA

The Genius CPA knows that it is improtant to stay in regular contact with people who sign up at their website.

INSIGHT

Some of them will decide they are not interested and will unsubscribe. But if they are not interested, you don't want them on your list anyways.

You will need to decide how often you want to send an email and the type of information you wish to send. For example, you may want to issue a regular newsletter or simply send emails that contain relevant information.

Whatever approach and timing you choose, you should be providing them with valuable information that helps build your reputation.

We'll cover this in more detail in the chapter on profitable relationships.

SOCIAL MEDIA STRATEGIES

More and more professional practices are now seeing the power of social media as a way of promoting their practice and connecting with clients and prospects.

However the field is developing so fast that it can be hard to know where to start. It can also be a huge drain on your time if you are not careful about it.

Some of the advantages of getting involved with social media are that it can help you:

- Establish a brand.

- Connect easily with large numbers of people.

- Build a reputation for expertise in your area.

- Create a two-way dialogue with your clients and prospects.

There are a few important points to consider:

1. Choose Where You Want To Be Seen

There is a growing range of social media outlets and it is therefore important to choose the most suitable for your needs. Currently the three most popular are:

- **Facebook**, which has more than 500 million users around the world. While it is widely used by businesses, some see it more for personal contacts.

- **Twitter** is a way of sharing quick updates with a large number of people. It can be good for making contacts as you can reach out to anyone.

- **LinkedIn** is a growing business network where you can make contact with a wide range of possible clients and partners.

Google Plus is also growing in importance and seems set to be a major force in this field.

Other aspects of social media include:

- Sharing videos on YouTube and other video sites.

- Sharing pictures on Flickr and similar sites.

- Sharing valuable links on social bookmarking sites such as Digg and StumbleUpon.

The key to making the most of these opportunities is sharing valuable information that interests people. It doesn't matter whether it's personal, funny, controversial or business-related, you want to be sharing information that people find interesting.

2. Get Involved

If you're going to get involved in social media, it's important to commit some time to building relationships and maintaining contact.

In your personal information, you want to come across as an interesting person whom people would want to make contact with. That may involve sharing some personal stuff as well as purely professional information.

The first step in the social marketing process is usually connecting with people you already know and then reaching out through their contacts to meet other people. You can also target specific people that you want to connect with.

If you're going to connect with people, you need to give them a reason to stay in touch. That means interacting and sharing valuable information.

You never know when an online contact could turn into a valuable business relationship.

3. Manage Your Time

While social networking can be extremely valuable, there is a risk that it can absorb too much of your time.

There are various tools that help you automate elements of it and make the most of your time.

Some examples are:

- TweetDeck which allows you to keep track of your Twitter, Facebook, and LinkedIn activity all in one place.

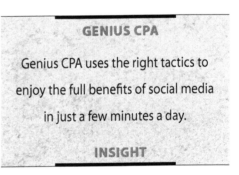

GENIUS CPA

Genius CPA uses the right tactics to enjoy the full benefits of social media in just a few minutes a day.

INSIGHT

- HootSuite which allows you to be more productive by carrying out many social media tasks in one location.

You can also benefit from outsourcing or delegating some of your social media tasks.

A valuable book that I recommend on this topic is:

- *Social Media Strategies for Professionals and Their Firms* by Michelle Golden

 **Identify your objectives for using social media and develop a plan for doing it effectively.**

TRACKING AND ANALYTICS

Successful online marketing requires commitment of time and money and it's important to always be looking for ways to give yourself a better return.

That means it's essential to track and measure the results you achieve.

Most practice owners don't have a clear idea of what results they're getting from their website. If you have no measurable data, you don't know whether it's performing well or needs improvement.

If you know that thirty of every hundred people that visit your site sign up for your email list, you can take action to improve on that.

Here are some of the pertinent facts you need to track:

- The number of people visiting your website.

- The length of time they stay and which pages they visit.

- How many of the visitors sign up for your email list.

- Where people come to your website from.

- Keywords they are using to reach it.

Most web hosting companies provide some degree of website analysis, but a much better option is to install tracking software, such as the free Google Analytics. This gives you access to a lot of data and can normally be added to your website quite easily.

 **Ensure you have good analytics software installed on your website and take action to monitor the data.**

RECOMMENDED RESOURCES TO IMPROVE YOUR ONLINE MARKETING

Here are some useful resources to help you get better results from online marketing:

Blogging

www.wordpress.org

Publishing Articles Online

www.ezinearticles.com
www.articlesbase.com
www.buzzle.com

Publishing Press Releases Online

www.prweb.com

Keyword Research

https://adwords.google.com/select/KeywordToolExternal

Local Search

www.google.com/lbc

Social Media Management

www.tweetdeck.com
www.hootsuite.com

Online Advertising

www.google.com/adwords

Tracking and Analytics

www.google.com/analytics

Powerful Online Presence:
TOP MISTAKES TO AVOID

Here are common mistakes that cause CPAs to miss out on the benefits of online marketing:

- **Wasted web design.** Spending too much time and money on flashy design and gimmicks can be counter-productive. It is not only distracting but could result in your site not being able to be viewed in some web browsers.

- **Failing to collect email addresses.** Most visitors will only hit your site once, so you need to ask for their contact details – and make the request clear and prominent.

- **Not driving traffic.** With billions of websites out there, people won't find yours on their own. You need to take steps to attract visitors.

- **Not encouraging feedback and comments.** A modern website is a two-way communication channel and is a great way to find out what your targeted audience see as important.

- **Not tracking and testing.** The internet makes it easy to test different marketing methods so you should always be trying new approaches to see what works best.

- **Wasting money on advertising.** There are many free ways to drive traffic to your website and there is often no need to spend money on advertising.

- **Not integrating online and offline.** Online channels don't stand alone and you should link them to your offline activity.

- **Failing to capture attention.** People's attention spans are very short online and you need to use a combination of powerful headlines, clear design and good writing to attract and hold their interest.

KEYS TO SUCCESS

- Building Your Online Home
  - Establish a clear purpose
  - Keep it simple
  - Grab their attention
  - Keep asking for their details
  - Make sure the site is visitor-friendly

- Driving Traffic to Your Website
  - Search Engine Optimization
  - Local Search
  - Advertising Online
  - Articles
  - Press Releases
  - Video Marketing
  - Offline Activity

- Turning Visitors into Clients

- Social Media Strategies
  - Choose where you want to be seen
  - Get involved
  - Manage your time

- Analytics and Tracking

Make a note of the additional key points from this chapter and what actions you plan to take as a result.

6
PROFITABLE CLIENT RELATIONSHIPS:
Growing Your Profits the Easy Way By Getting Closer to Existing Clients

----

"In marketing I've seen only one strategy that can't miss – you market to your best customers first, your best prospects second, and the rest of the world last."

JOHN ROMERO
ENTREPRENEUR AND GAMES DESIGNER

THIS MAY SEEM LIKE a strange thing to say in a book about growing your practice, but I believe that one of the biggest marketing mistakes made by many CPAs is that they put too much effort into winning new clients.

Now, of course, I'm not saying you shouldn't be taking action to get new clients. In this book, I share many strategies for doing exactly that. However, what I want to emphasize is that, sometimes, in the rush to get new clients, we forget to pay adequate attention to our existing ones.

The Genius CPA knows that, having succeeded in winning a new client, you have to put extra effort not only into holding on to that client, but also into encouraging them to expand the range of services for which they hire you.

There is a great deal of research which shows that it costs much less to sell more to an existing client than it does to win a new one – in fact, I've read reports that state it can be five or six times more expensive to attract new clients.

Building on Existing Commitment

Existing clients are naturally your best bet for building additional revenue.

- They know you already.

- They have made a commitment to you.

- You should be in regular contact with them.

In this chapter, we'll discuss strategies for keeping in touch and fostering relationships.

The key to building a successful practice is to have the right balance and make sure you have strategies in place both to attract new clients and to create more profitable relationships with existing clients.

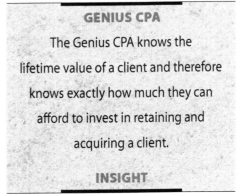

GENIUS CPA

The Genius CPA knows the lifetime value of a client and therefore knows exactly how much they can afford to invest in retaining and acquiring a client.

INSIGHT

I know that some practitioners find it difficult to see how they can make more money from existing clients as they feel they offer a limited range of services.

So, in the next chapter, we'll look at how you can increase your income through changing your fee structure, reviewing the packaging of your services and developing and cross-selling additional offers.

However, you can't just do a good job and assume your clients will stay with you and engage you for more services.

**You need to put in place a strategy for building
and deepening relationships to ensure that clients
are open to buying additional services.**

This is a process that begins right from your very first contact with a prospect and continues by strengthening trust over time so that the relationship becomes mutually profitable. In this chapter, I'll cover seven proven strategies you can use to build closer relationships with your prospects and clients.

But first, we need to understand the importance of knowing how much each client is worth.

KNOWING HOW MUCH EACH CLIENT IS WORTH

Knowing how much a client is worth to you is one of the most important numbers in your practice.

But it's surprising how many CPAs don't know what this number is – never mind having a strategy in place for increasing it.

The best way to measure how much a client is worth is to calculate their LTV (lifetime value). This is simply the amount of money they would pay you during their time as one of your clients. It is calculated as follows:

Lifetime Value = T x M

T = Time in years a client will stay with you
M = Amount they will spend with you each year

So, for example, if a typical client pays $4,000 per year in fees for various services and they will retain you for an average of 5 years, their lifetime value to you is 5 x $4,000 = $20,000.

Knowing that information helps you in several ways:

- Shows how much you can afford to spend to attract a client.

- Tells how much you can spend to prevent an existing client from going to a competitor.

- Gives you an incentive to keep them longer as a client.

- Emphasizes the importance of selling them more services to increase the total value.

 **Calculate the LTV of your typical client using the T x M formula.**

WHAT YOU CAN AFFORD TO INVEST

So, if an average good client is worth $20,000 to you, how much would you be prepared to spend to attract a new client?

Whenever I ask CPA practitioners how much they'd be willing to spend to bring in a new client, I get an astounding response that usually ranges from $25 to $300.

Now maybe the amount is low because they are not charging the right fees or because client retention is a problem, hence the LTV of their client is nowhere close to where it should be. However, it is often because they don't understand the marketing game.

> **The marketing game is about finding the right marketing methods to bring in new clients where the ratio of marketing cost to LTV is attractive.**

You might happily spend $200 to bring in a client that is worth $20,000. But you may be equally as happy to spend $500 or $1,000.

You will need to decide what is acceptable for you, but when a client is going to be worth $20,000 over five years, you can probably afford to spend more than $25 to $300 to bring them in.

Time and time again, I find CPAs under-invest when it comes to acquiring new clients.

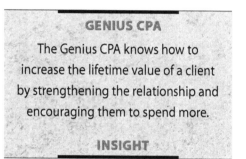

GENIUS CPA

The Genius CPA knows how to increase the lifetime value of a client by strengthening the relationship and encouraging them to spend more.

INSIGHT

However, once you have clients on board, you should be equally willing to invest time and money on deepening the relationship and keeping them.

Being able to keep a client for six years rather than four years is worth a great deal of revenue to your practice, so it is worth setting aside resources to help with client retention and relationship building.

Decide how much you can spend to bring in a new client. Decide how much you can spend to retain existing clients.

SEVEN WAYS TO BUILD RELATIONSHIPS WITH CLIENTS SO THEY SPEND MORE

In the next chapter, I'll talk about the specific steps you should take to make sure you are charging the appropriate level of fees and also how you should package and cross-sell your services to encourage clients to spend more with you.

For now, I want to focus on what you can do to stay in touch with your clients and build your relationship with them.

You may think your clients only want to hear from you when something needs to be done. But nothing could be further from the truth. They see you as an important advisor (if they are not, refer to Chapter 3 to learn how to position yourself as an expert) and they expect you to keep in touch and keep them informed.

Research shows that the single biggest reason small business owners change their CPA is because the CPA doesn't stay in touch with them.

You can have the best marketing system in the world for bringing in new clients but, if you don't have a system in place for building relationships with your clients, you will not have much growth.

My coaching member Roy Fisher, CPA says new clients who come on board with his firm routinely say they did not hear from their prior CPA enough. They know they need their CPA's point of view on financial matters and they didn't get it as often as they wanted.

He believes the typical CPA is backed up with so much work and client demands that they think they don't have time to communicate effectively with their client base.

But he argues that you need to make time to communicate with clients and potential clients.

He says his firm is just beginning to scratch the surface with client communication.

They have already implemented print newsletters and are developing new and innovative ways to communicate with their clients and potential clients. They are starting to use all media types, including email, video and audio to do so.

He adds: "Our clients are closer to us than they ever were before but when all of our communication methods are fully functioning, we will not lose a client to a competitor ever again unless we fire them."

If you don't keep in touch, the Lifetime Value of each client will be much lower due to client attrition and you will have to spend more of your time and money on getting new clients.

Here are seven strategies you can use to deepen your relationship with clients and prospects:

1. PUBLISH A PRINTED MONTHLY NEWSLETTER

One of the best ways of establishing consistent client contact is through a printed client newsletter. I would go as far as to say that this is a *must have* for growing your practice.

I know a lot of CPAs feel they get poor results from using newsletters. But the reason they get poor results is that they use "canned" newsletters, where someone else provides all the content, which is usually, from my observation, dry and boring.

A couple of CPA practitioners recently told me they had stopped their client newsletter subscription because it didn't work. I had to agree this was the right decision because canned newsletters simply don't deliver results. It's just throwing money down the drain.

The whole point of a newsletter is to build the relationship between you and your clients and you can't do that when someone else is creating generic content that is for the most part technical in nature and uninteresting to read.

On the other hand, when you send a customized and well-crafted newsletter to all your clients and prospects, it can be a very powerful tool.

It can help you increase client retention, cross-sell other services, obtain more referrals, and convert prospects to clients.

Here are three ways you benefit from having a strong client newsletter:

- **Builds an "iron fence."** The chances are that another CPA is trying to lure your clients away right now. You need to build an iron fence around your clients. You can do this by offering relevant, useful and entertaining value through a regular newsletter.

- **Deepens relationships.** Strong relationships grow out of being an ongoing fixture in your client's life. Relationships are built on trust and regular contact. A newsletter is an important part of this process.

- **Adds the power of personality.** Although people think accountants are boring (the public perception is probably right up there with IT guys), we don't have to behave that way. I've found that the most successful professional firms have a distinct identity and personality. A newsletter is an easy way to show these unique qualities.

A good newsletter really can serve multiple purposes. And, when you do it well, it helps to position you as an expert.

> **Your newsletter is an opportunity to reinforce your central marketing message and is an easy way to increase your number of contacts with each client per year.**

This helps you to retain clients.

In addition, you may find that your newsletters are being passed around and get into the hands of prospective clients you haven't yet identified – for example if a client leaves copies in their waiting room.

One of the features I include in my client newsletter is a "Client of the Month" which includes a profile of the client's business and a photograph. Most people appreciate being featured in this way and it often leads to business for them when they are contacted by other readers.

I often get clients asking how they can be featured in that part of the newsletter.

Superstar member Bob Goodman, CPA has enjoyed great results from my monthly print newsletter service – and particularly from including a client of the month in the newsletter he sends to his respective list.

He had been sending out tax newsletters for more than twenty-five years, but had not seen a great deal of response. Yet that changed completely when he introduced the newsletter service I've made available.

He says: "When I included a client of the month, I started receiving feedback every week. To my surprise, everyone wanted to be client of the month. They also enjoy the jokes and the style of the newsletter."

He advises all CPAs to include a client of the month in their newsletters and to send out as many as possible to existing clients, bankers, brokers and all referral sources.

High Return on Low Investment

Producing a newsletter can provide a remarkable return on investment. Printing and mailing each issue should cost you less than $2 per client – meaning the total cost is less than $25 a year (per client) for a monthly newsletter.

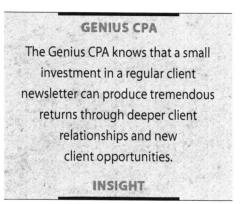

GENIUS CPA

The Genius CPA knows that a small investment in a regular client newsletter can produce tremendous returns through deeper client relationships and new client opportunities.

INSIGHT

Here are just a few examples of the returns I got from that investment in just one year.

- Three months after I started mailing my newsletter to a list of local businesses, I received a call from the owner of one of the businesses on that list. Within two weeks, this business was on board as my client, with annual fees totaling $16,000 in the first year. Three years later, that business had paid my firm a total of $68,250. My investment of $25 in sending a newsletter returned $68,250 in revenue.

- A client who responded to a newsletter offer signed up

immediately and paid $5,400 in fees the first year and $6,500 for the three following years. My $25 investment in this client returned $24,900 in revenue.

- A long-time client of mine shared my newsletter with one of his vendors who then became one of my top-paying clients, paying in excess of $15,000 in fees per year. Taking into account additional services, in the three years since they signed up, they have paid more than $105,000 in fees – all as a result of my $25 investment in sending a newsletter to my client.

Altogether, from an investment of around $75, I earned more than $198,150 in new revenue.

On top of that, I know many clients renew their service contract with my firm year after year because of the regular contact they receive from us, of which the newsletter is an important part.

Just one referral that Bob Goodman got from a lawyer as a direct result of his newsletter was worth more than $10,000 in fees from a new client. I am totally convinced that the time spent on producing a newsletter is a worthwhile investment. Yet the commitment required to produce a great newsletter does not have to be huge.

I know many of my members have had similar results from issuing their own newsletters.

Superstar member Eric Nelson, CPA believes that one of the keys to the success of his newsletter was learning to communicate with clients in his own voice, rather than using off-the-shelf newsletters.

He says: "My clients know me and they know how I speak. Using the verbiage I normally use builds trust in that they know the newsletter was written by me."

He adds that one of the advantages of writing his own newsletter is that he can answer common questions that many of his clients are asking in one shot.

Instead of having to call *all* the clients back individually, he covers them all in a simple newsletter article.

He points out a further benefit: "It's another way of staying in touch with my clients and prospects in a way that nobody else in my market does. That builds trust and differentiation."

Below are my Top Ten Tips for producing an effective client newsletter.

TOP TEN TIPS FOR CREATING A GREAT CLIENT NEWSLETTER

1. **Brief:** Quality is more important than quantity – you don't need 12 pages (or 100 for that matter; after all, it's not a manifesto). A short four page newsletter is fine, especially to get started. You can easily expand it later if you wish.

2. **Simple**: You don't need a flashy, glossy design. It doesn't even have to be full color. I create mine in Word on my computer, and then send it to my graphics person and then to my printer. It costs me very little and, as you have just read, the return on your investment, both in terms of time and money, is huge.

3. **Regular**: I suggest you send it every month. Frequency is important.

4. **Educational:** Don't go for too much sales pitch. Share information that people find useful and that they look forward to receiving. That way, you are giving the client or prospective client something of value for free, and also establishing yourself as an expert in your field.

5. **Fun:** Keep it business-like, but make it enjoyable to read. Avoid being boring. If your client wanted to be bored they could read the back of the cereal box! That means you can include jokes, funny stories and cartoons, just be sure to use your judgment and keep it tasteful and non-offensive.

6. **Accurate**: As it's about establishing your reputation, make sure you check your facts and don't rely soley on your spell checker. Have someone proofread it for you and be especially careful with dates and numbers.

7. **Consistent:** Keep the layout, format and topics consistent from issue to issue so that people get used to seeing it.

8. **Easy to Read:** Avoid too much fancy design and strange colors or typefaces. Have plenty of white space to increase readability and make it easier on your readers' eyes.

9. **Topical**: Where possible, include current news and information so that people see it as a valuable source of up-to-date knowledge.

10. **Participative**: Feature your clients with testimonials and case studies – you can even ask them to contribute.

Here is how my firm's newsletter is structured:

1. Welcome

2. Main article

3. **New tax laws or a tax reduction strategy**

4. **Client feedback / testimonial**

5. **Ask for referral or cross-sell other services**

6. **Humor / jokes / short interesting articles on a variety of topics**

7. Q & A

To make it easy to create the content, I set up a series of manila file folders for each of these topics and, whenever I see something interesting, I put it into one of these folders for future reference.

Remember, the newsletter is both about building your relationship with existing clients and reaching out to new ones. So make sure you build a large mailing list to reach as many people as possible.

For a limited number of practices which want to produce a high-quality newsletter with minimum work, my Genius CPA Newsletter Service may be of interest. See the description that follows for more information.

 **Choose a name and frequency for your newsletter and then outline the topics you want to cover. Create and issue your first newsletter.**

Recommended Resource: Genius CPA Newsletter Service

While publishing a print newsletter has worked amazingly well for me and for other CPAs, issuing one on a regular basis isn't necessarily easy. You have to pull together resources in copywriting, design, printing and mailing. So, even though the return makes it well worth the effort, you may not have the time to get your newsletter off the ground. The good news is that my Genius CPA Newsletter Service will take the hassle and legwork off your hands.

Here's what you can expect every single month as a member:

- **Ready-to-mail newsletter:** Four-page print newsletter, ready for you to print and mail to your clients.

- **Make it your own:** Send us your picture, logo and contact info and we'll send you a finished newsletter, complete with your customized information.

- **Add your own articles:** We've set aside two areas you can use to include your own articles – though we'll include substitutes if you prefer.

Your four-page "Straight Talk About Small Business Success" newsletter is built around my proven model.

Along with your newsletter, you'll also get these two valuable bonuses:

#1: Training Audio walking you through the newsletter process.

#2: Marketing Strategies Audio on using your newsletter to grow your practice.

For more information, visit:

www.ToEnrollNow.com

2. SEND PERSONAL CARDS AND GIFTS

Sometimes simple personal touches can have the biggest effect. Sending clients a card on their birthday or on a holiday can make a big impact.

Everyone likes to receive a personal message and these days the shift to email and electronic communication means this often gets forgotten.

A thank you card when someone does something you appreciate can also go a long way. For example, if you send someone a card or note to thank them for a referral, they'll probably give you another referral. These messages must be personalized and ideally handwritten to have the best impression possible.

It's also a good idea to send an appropriate gift on occasions as well – such as on birthdays or holidays. I advise CPAs to spend up to 5% of their revenues on gifts to clients.

A $20,000 value client is surely worth the investment of a few dollars in a suitable gift!

Florida CPA Steven R. Press says his practice has had a great response by using this approach.

His firm sends clients birthday cards and many of them call the office to say thank you.

When they sign up a new client, they send a UPS delivery of a gourmet popcorn tin, with a personal note, which the clients really enjoy – and they do the same for some top clients at holiday time.

> **GENIUS CPA**
>
> The Genius CPA appreciates new clients and people who give them referrals – and they let them know with a "Thank You."
>
> **INSIGHT**

In addition, they give movie tickets to people who refer new clients.

 **Identify opportunities to send cards or gifts to clients.**

3. ISSUE A WEEKLY EMAIL NEWSLETTER OR EZINE

As well as sending a monthly print newsletter by mail, you should consider sending your clients and prospects a regular email newsletter – known as an ezine.

This is a special email you send to your list weekly, semi-weekly or monthly giving them information you feel will be useful to them.

You'll find that some people will prefer to get emails and others prefer to read printed newsletters. Some will read both.

However, you shouldn't expect everyone on your list to read every item you send them. That's why you need to build a series of touch points that allow people to hear from you in different ways.

I have often met with business owners that were not ready to come aboard with my firm for one reason or another at the time of my initial meeting.

However, I would add them to my ezine list so that they then receive something from me on a weekly basis.

I am fairly confident that their existing CPA was not keeping in touch with them and this simple act of sending them snippets of information can convert a prospect into a client over a period of time.

I use a program called Infusionsoft for building and managing my list. This is quite an advanced system with a lot of customer relationship capability but not everyone needs such a full service.

Other popular choices among professional firms for managing email lists are Constant Contact and Aweber.

Many of the principles for setting up an ezine are similar to those for setting up a printed newsletter – the main difference being that it is not printed and mailed out.

Here are a few tips for creating an effective ezine:

- **The subject line is key.** The subject line of your email will have a big impact on whether people even open it, so make sure it gives a strong reason to open the email.

- **Test different approaches.** Most email systems make it easy to find out the impact of different approaches such as using different headlines to see what works best.

- **Choose between HTML and text.** Some people prefer the simplicity of a text based message while others feel the more professional look of an HTML email is better.

- **Be consistent.** Follow a regular schedule and while it is fine to test different approaches, the general format and type of content should stay the same between issues so that people know what to expect.

- **Deliver valuable information.** If people feel you are spamming them with irrelevant content that is selling too hard, they will unsubscribe and you will miss out on a potential client.

 **Create a plan for issuing a regular ezine.**

4. KEEP IN TOUCH WITH REGULAR EMAIL

In addition to using your email list to send out regular newsletters, you can set it up to send out messages at specific intervals.

So, for example, you may want to have a series of timed messages going out to people who have just signed up for your list. This can tell them a bit more about your firm, your people and the services you provide.

While you don't want to be sending people too many emails, you need to maintain regular contact by providing valuable information.

As well as using automated emails, don't forget to send personal emails to people as well – perhaps attaching an article you wrote or read or sending a summary of a useful book you have just finished reading.

 **Identify opportunities to send specific emails to clients.**

5. MAINTAIN PERSONAL CONTACT

According to Kevin Hogan's book *Psychology of Persuasion*, people are more likely to do what you ask if they believe you have their best interests in mind. This is the "Law of Friends."

Building a business relationship means you have to show clients that you are looking after their interests and this trust is something that can only be built over time.

You can do this by taking an interest in your clients as people. *Built to Last* author Jim Collins says: "Don't be interesting. Be interested."

Doing that helps you think of people as individuals. To learn about them, you need to listen to them. The more you know about their likes and dislikes, the more personal you can make your services. This allows you to send them clippings you know will interest them or to recognize their personal achievements and family events.

Here are some ways you can make a valued customer feel special:

- Using their name.

- Talking with them about non-business topics.

- Informing them early about your new services.

- Responding quickly to their calls and emails.

These seemingly small things can start to build the chemistry of a profitable long-term relationship.

The more you know about someone's life outside of work, the more you can talk about their family and interests, making them feel unique and special rather than part of a large group.

Depending on the client and your relationship, you may include personal visits in the schedule. My choice is normally not to do this, but others choose differently.

What you do is less important than the fact that you are making it personal.

 **Make a plan for personal contact with clients.**

6. ACQUIRE THE RIGHT SOFTWARE TO MANAGE AND DEVELOP RELATIONSHIPS

If you want to build close relationships with customers and prospects, you need to take great care to keep your database clean, up to date and meaningfully segmented.

Keeping an effective database is about a lot more than having correct names and addresses – if that was all there was to it, any phone book would suffice. If you are about to call someone, wouldn't it be helpful to know – or have a reminder – that they have just had a new addition to the family or a divorce or they've been on holiday.

Being able to make a few appropriate personal comments or ask the right questions can make a big difference when establishing a personal relationship. They don't know you've just read it off your database; they just care that you took the time to comment.

Clearly this is most valuable as your practice gets larger and you have more staff dealing with the same client. But even in a smaller firm, it's useful to have reliable up-to-date records.

There are many good Customer Relationship Management software programs around – including Infusionsoft, as I mentioned. Some other names to check out are ACT and Goldmine.

Even Outlook works as a CRM resource and there are now many web-based services available online.

We have various groups set up like this:

- Business accounting clients.

- Personal tax clients for the current year.

- Prospects who ordered my special report.

- Prospects segmented by profession, e.g. dentists, chiropractors.

As well as taking time to find the right software for your needs, make sure that someone on your team knows how to use it to its full advantage.

Then make a commitment to keeping it up to date as any database is only as good as the data within it.

 **Identify and acquire the right software for CRM and email software.**

7. USE YOUR EMAIL SIGNATURE AS A MARKETING TOOL

Your email signature is a remarkably powerful client attraction tool that can help you connect with new people and build relationships with current contacts.

When you enable the "signature" feature in your email program, this allows you to create a short message that goes out at the bottom of every email you send. The message should be relatively short and should contain:

- Your name and the name of your firm.

- Your tagline, USP or competitive advantage.

- Website address.

For example, here is mine:

Salim Omar, CPA, MBA
Author: *Straight Talk About Small Business Success in New Jersey,* now available in all Barnes and Noble bookstores and on Amazon.com
President: The Omar Group, CPA
49 Cliffwood Avenue, Suite 200, Cliffwood, NJ 07721
Website: www.OmarGroupCPA.com
Fax: (732) 566-3565
Telephone: (732) 566-3660

 **Create your email signature and start using it.**

YOUR CLIENT TOUCH PLAN

As I mentioned earlier, the biggest complaint of many clients is that their CPA does not keep in touch with them.

In this chapter, I have shared many ways you can easily rectify that and keep in touch with your clients. However, in order to do that, you will need to develop a plan.

Over the course of a year, I recommend that you should be in touch with each of your clients at least 24 times.

For my CPA practice, it is more like 60-70 times per year!

This breaks down as follows:

Monthly newsletter	12
Birthday card or gift	1
Anniversary of business relationship	1
Thanksgiving card	1
Thank you postcard	2
Weekly ezine	52
Personal visits	1
Personal phone calls	2

That's 60-70 touches per year.

On the following page, I have given an example of a full year's touch plan. These are touches in addition to monthly newsletters and weekly ezines.

EXAMPLE: CLIENT TOUCH PLAN

January	Email #1 (with Happy New Year wishes) Referral Request Letter
February	Email #2 & Email #3
March	A short note with an article you read or a book summary Email #4 & Email #5
April	Email #6 After tax-season to check in
May	Email #7 Book read with important points you walked away with
June	An interesting article with a handwritten note Email #8
July	Email #9 Birthday card
August	Book read with important points you walked away with Email #10
September	Referral postcard Email #11
October	Email #12
November	Thanksgiving card Email #13
December	Phone call to wish Happy Holidays Email #14

RECOMMENDED RESOURCES: CLIENT RELATIONSHIPS

Here are some useful resources to help you get better client relationships:

Sending Out Personalized Cards
www.SendOutCards.com

Customer Relationship Software
ACT
Goldmine

Email and Ezine Software
www.Aweber.com
www.ConstantContact.com
www.Infusionsoft.com

Profitable Client Relationships:
TOP MISTAKES TO AVOID

Here are common mistakes that get in the way of making the most of client relationships:

- **Not knowing your LTV.** Most CPAs don't know the true Lifetime Value of a client to them and therefore they tend to underspend on acquiring and retaining clients.

- **Using "canned" newsletters.** Many CPAs have been disappointed with the results they get from pre-prepared newsletters, but a good newsletter has to be seen to come from you.

- **Failing to stay in touch with clients.** The biggest reason why people change CPA firms is that they don't hear often enough from their current CPA. Just keeping in touch with clients puts you in a better position.

- **Having an ineffective newsletter.** Even though many firms don't bother publishing a newsletter, many of those that do, end up failing because they are too boring, issued irregularly or don't focus on the client.

- **Not staying in touch by email.** Lots of businesses collect email addresses and then never use them to follow up. They are missing out on a valuable and easy way to build their reputation and deepen relationships.

- **Forgetting the personal touch.** Amongst all the use of technology, it is easy to forget that a handwritten card or personal phone call counts for a great deal.

- **Not having a client touch plan.** Without a carefully crafted contact plan, you end up not finding the time to stay in touch.

KEYS TO SUCCESS

- The Lifetime Value of your clients is one of the most valuable pieces of information in your practice. Knowing this helps you work out how much you can afford to spend to attract and retain clients.

- You need to develop a regular contact program – involving at least 24 touches per year – to help build a closer relationship with your clients.

- You have to invest in the right software for managing your email contacts and also for tracking your overall customer relationships.

- Creating a personalized print newsletter is one of the best ways for establishing your expertise and staying in touch with clients and prospects.

- Supplementing this with an email ezine helps to reach out in other ways.

- It is important to make sure that some of your communication with your top clients is personal – either through personal contact, cards or emails.

Make a note of the additional key points from this chapter and what actions you are going to take as a result.

7
PRICING AND PACKAGING:
Secrets to Ensuring Your Clients and Prospects Will Happily Pay More for Your Services

----

"Until you value yourself, you will not value your time. Until you value your time, you will not do anything with it."

M. Scott Peck
Author: *The Road Less Travelled*
1936 – 2005

THERE IS ONE SIMPLE change you can make in your practice that could result in tens of thousands of additional dollars in your pocket this year!

That change is making sure that you are charging appropriately for your services.

Undercharging has a negative impact on the profitability of your practice and take-home pay. It is a very common problem that I see amongst many practices.

When I recently interviewed Jason Marrs, the co-author (with Dan Kennedy) of *No B.S. Price Strategy: The Ultimate No Holds Barred, Kick Butt, Take No Prisoners Guide to Profits, Power, and Prosperity*, he explained the mental barriers that most business owners are faced with when trying to raise prices and fees.

He said that one of the mental barriers, and the #1 enemy of maximum profitability, is commodity thinking.

I've already talked about the problems of commoditization, but the added insight from Jason is that he argues there is no such thing as a commodity; there is only *commodity thinking*.

To prove his point, he backed it up by sharing real life examples of two items, water and air, that we think of as commodities. You could argue that it's impossible to get more commoditized than these because they are available for free and there is no need to buy them.

Yet both are now sold at premium prices in the market place.

During the interview, Jason offers a lot of non-traditional advice on how to go about conquering this mindset.

> Download the full interview with pricing expert Jason Marrs
> titled "Common Mistakes Practitioners Make With the Fees They Charge
> and How to Avoid Them!" as part of the Reader-Only Special Bonus
> at www.TheUltimateCPAPractice.com/free.html

Maximizing Lifetime Value

As I mentioned in the last chapter, one of the most important numbers in your practice is the Lifetime Value of your clients. One of the main factors that drives Lifetime Value is how much revenue you generate from the work you do for a client in the course of a year.

The fees you charge will determine how much you make, but too many CPA firms limit the Lifetime Value and end up with thin profit margins because they underprice their services.

They are often tempted to cut their rates because they think that is the way to attract more clients and generate increased revenue. They scramble to slash their fees below the levels charged by their competitors and end up doing more work for less revenue.

This takes the firm into a death spiral that ultimately leads to failure.

As Paul Dunn and Ron Baker highlight in "*The Firm of the Future*":

CPAs should price for profitability and not for market share.

What that means is that you are likely to be more profitable having 100 clients paying you $10,000 a year than you would be having 1,000 clients paying you $1,000 a year.

Right-sizing Fees

Right after this past tax season, my senior manager went through the process of examining all of our business clients and right-sizing them for the services we provide.

As you know, a client's business changes with time – they may add more bank accounts, have more transactions in each bank account, add more employees, have new loans, etc. This means more work for us, the accounting firm.

To demonstrate how important and rewarding this exercise is, I'll share with you the impact it will have on my practice this year.

After this fairly simple task of right-sizing, my practice will generate an additional $38,000 in annual fees and most of it will be contributing to the bottom line.

Over a five year period, that equates to nearly $200,000! Not bad at all.

You can see why it is so important to charge the appropriate amount for your services.

Steps to Success

In this section, I'll cover the essential steps you need to follow to make sure you are charging correctly for your services and maximizing the Lifetime Value of your clients. They are:

- Pricing your services based on the value you deliver.

- Packaging services to allow for higher profit through increased fees and longer-term relationships.

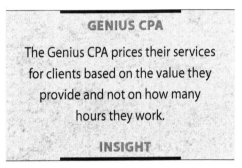

GENIUS CPA

The Genius CPA prices their services for clients based on the value they provide and not on how many hours they work.

INSIGHT

- Promoting and cross-selling a wider range of offers to your clients.

We'll cover each of these steps in subsequent pages. But first of all, there is one key issue that all CPAs need to face up to – that is the fact that too many have bought into the idea that the best way to charge for their service is using an hourly rate.

WHY HOURLY RATES ARE DETRIMENTAL FOR YOU AND YOUR CLIENTS

One of the biggest problems we face as a profession is that practices have taken their collective intellectual capital and commoditized it into a one-dimensional billing rate. This is a serious mistake both from profitability and marketing standpoints.

The benefits you give to your clients deserve much more thought and creativity than merely a rate multiplied by hours.

There is a famous story of a large factory where one of the most important pieces of machinery failed. The owners were desperate to have it fixed as it was costing them a huge amount of money to have it out of action.

They called on all their experts to try and get it working, but nobody seemed to know what to do. Eventually one man turned up with a large bag of tools and looked over the machine.

After inspecting it, he reached into his bag and pulled out a small hammer. He gently tapped the machine in a few places and quickly it sprung into life.

The owners were initially delighted, but then they were shocked the following week to receive a bill for $10,000.

They thought it must be a mistake and sent him a message saying it was unreasonable as he had only been there less than one hour and had not done much. So they politely asked for an itemized bill. They received the following.

To inspecting machine and tapping with hammer:	$100
To knowing where to tap:	$9,900
Total:	$10,000

In truth, the value of the work he did for them was much more than the amount he billed because it enabled them to recover their lost revenue. However, they were stuck on the idea that the value of work was measured by the number of hours it took.

The truth is that exactly the same applies in our field. When you allow people to get the idea that value is measured by hours of work, you undercharge for what you deliver.

You need to find a way to move your own thinking – and that of your clients – on to a different platform.

HOW TO PRICE YOUR SERVICES BASED ON VALUE

The primary goal of your firm's marketing strategy should *not* be to acquire revenue at any price. It should be to gain the largest possible share of highly *profitable* work.

In order to do that, you need to move the conversation with the prospective client on to value, not the number of hours it will take to get the job done.

One of the best resources I've come across on the subject of creating value is *The Strategy & Tactics of Pricing: A Guide to Profitable Decision Making* by Thomas Nagle and Reed Holden.

This outlines what they call the five C's of value:

1. **Comprehend** what drives sustainable value for customers.

2. **Create** value for customers.

3. **Communicate** the value that you create.

4. **Convince** customers that they must pay for value received.

5. **Capture** value with appropriate price metrics and fences.

This means it is not enough to price based upon a client's willingness and ability to pay. You must increase that willingness by constantly communicating the value of your services.

Every job for every customer has value drivers, and your job is to understand what those are.

In my practice, I use fees as a way to keep track of how much value I'm delivering to my clients.

When we are charging higher fees, it means my clients are getting the maximum value the practice has to offer. My team views our premium fees as a clear signal that we are truly the best in the business and we have paying clients to prove it!

When you charge higher fees, you will attract premium clients, be able to recruit and retain high-caliber staff, and even cut back on the hours you put in at the office!

It's a win-win for you and your clients.

So let's look at three steps you can take to begin increasing your fees:

1. DEVELOP THE RIGHT MINDSET FOR CHARGING MORE

The first step in changing your thinking about price is starting to view your fees as a marketing tool.

The reality is that your fees have a big influence on how clients and potential clients *value* your services. People will take your fees into account when judging your quality, expertise and success. Automobile companies such as Mercedes Benz, BMW and Lexus are good examples of companies that fetch a high price for their vehicles because they convey quality, craftsmanship, etc.

That's why genius practitioners continually adjust their fees upwards to reflect the premium value and service that they want to send to prospective clients.

If you believe that your practice delivers superior value you *must* charge accordingly.

If you are hesitant to charge what you are truly worth, then your clients will naturally resist paying it – they are not going to voluntarily offer to pay you more. If you are hesitant, you need to work out whether it is an issue about belief or an issue about the actual quality of your services.

If you are doing a good job for your clients, charging low fees is almost always a question of your belief.

You are the expert and you deliver smart solutions to your client's complex business problems. Most clients value this and want to pay you accordingly.

You should therefore never undercut your future profit and value by undercharging to get the business.

Like that engineer with his hammer, you should always charge based on the value of the solution you provide, not on the hours of work needed to deliver it!

Sometimes, the most important step towards charging higher fees is simply to decide what your new fees are and then inform your clients about them.

You Deserve Your Fees – Start Asking For Them!

2. DELIVER VALUE TO JUSTIFY HIGHER PRICING

The next step in the process of ensuring that you obtain premium fees for the service you provide is to position your practice so that you play an integral role in the success of your client's business.

Regardless of the service you provide, it has to be translated to the client as a value proposition.

If you own and operate a write-up practice, you'll never be seen to deliver true value if you are seen as the people who simply do the paperwork.

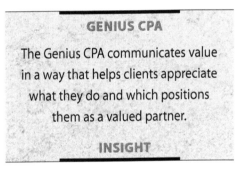

GENIUS CPA

The Genius CPA communicates value in a way that helps clients appreciate what they do and which positions them as a valued partner.

INSIGHT

Your clients want a seasoned professional who can provide them with friendly financial and tax advice in a way that is meaningful to a lay-person.

They also want someone to be their financial sounding board for their dreams and future plans. This is the real essence of your client relationships and what your fees actually pay for.

Your goal is to have your clients see you as an integral partner in the success of their business. When you achieve that, your fees are a secondary concern to them.

They will see themselves as paying for the relationship rather than a transaction. When you reach that point, you will be earning the fees you deserve.

Asking the Right Questions

To find out what the value proposition is for the services your firm provides, I recommend that you have a frank and open conversation with your clients about their business. You can do this by asking important questions such as:

1. What keeps you up at night?

2. What are your major challenges?

3. What are your long and short term growth plans?

4. Do you have a marketing plan and budget in place?

5. What differentiates you from your competitors?

6. Do you anticipate capital needs?

The answers to these questions will give you priceless insight into their innermost problems and needs. When you can help them solve these problems, you are on the path to consistently profitable engagements.

What you *don't* want is to be the "Wal-Mart" of your market, promising the lowest prices to everyone. The competition is just too fierce and the returns are too low.

The best strategy is to understand what your clients really want and then deliver a premium service to meet their needs. When you do this successfully, charging the premium fee is simple and rewarding!

A pivotal part of the process is that you have to establish the right fees and inform your clients about it.

You shouldn't be hesitant about asking for what you are worth.

I recently had a chance to see how the price discussion plays out from a *consumer's* standpoint. It brought home to me how so many business owners and sales people tend to undercharge because they have not strategically thought this through.

My wife and I wanted to build a huge, 1,000+ square-foot multi-tiered brick patio with a built-in kitchen at the back of my three-year-old 6,000-square-foot home in central Jersey.

When we were seeking proposals from contractors, it was a real education to observe how the majority of them submit estimates.

They tend to view the patio as a commodity, i.e., they talk in terms of its *size*, the *quality* of the pavers they use, the *quantity* of pavers needed and thus leading into the price of the patio.

Out of nine contractors we interviewed, only one took the time to *first* understand *why* we were considering building the patio and what our needs were as well as what our dreams were of what the patio would look like.

It was only after he had that information that he went into the rest of his presentation.

He then incorporated our dreams into his presentation, including the years of enjoyment we would get from our patio, the ROI we would get if we were ever to sell the house, and the memories we would leave behind.

He certainly wasn't the lowest proposal that we received but he secured the job because he understood us and our needs and we felt we connected.

Besides the mistake of thinking of the patio as a commodity, here are other mistakes I observed that many of these contractors made:

- Arriving in a battered-up truck.

- Having no testimonials from their happy and satisfied clients.

- Presenting a portfolio containing pictures of past jobs that was falling apart.

- Lacking follow up (email, phone call or letter) after meeting with them.

- Attempting to differentiate themselves and their company by stating that they were one of the few who used polymeric sand to cover the spaces between the pavers. It seems most, if not all of them, use this product.

- Asking us the wrong question: "How much did we want to spend on the patio?" instead of asking us about our dreams.

3. PROMOTE YOUR VALUE SO THAT CLIENTS RECOGNIZE IT

The reason top CPAs can charge premium fees is that they are periodically reinforcing the value of the services they provide to their clients.

They don't focus on the transaction or service they provide, they talk about the benefits they deliver.

For example, I never frame my services as simply preparing financial statements and tax returns. Instead, I market my ability to:

- Decipher complicated financial information.

- Deliver insight that leads to smart financial decisions.

Every client wants these benefits and is willing to invest in getting this insight on a regular basis.

At my firm, I label one of my services as "Financial and Tax Stewardship" meetings. Before I meet with the client, I prepare for the meeting by reviewing the client's financial statements and I put together a meeting agenda. You can see an example of a meeting agenda that follows.

After I meet with the client, I send them minutes of what transpired at the meeting. These minutes are a one to two page summary of the salient points discussed and action items. Clients love this type of a proactive service. This is an example of where clearly communicating value lays the foundation for higher fees.

I want to share with you one other secret that has enabled me to charge higher fees.

You may think that being readily available to clients and prospects is the best way to keep them happy. But the truth is that *scarcity* is an important factor in setting your fee expectations. Price is a function of supply and demand. The sought-after CPA with limited availability commands the highest fee. This means you should look for opportunities to communicate your "in demand" status. For example, never tell your clients that you have complete days free for appointments – always take the lead and insist on specific dates and times.

Also, as we'll discuss in more detail in the next chapter, testimonials are a powerful way to promote your value and increase demand for your services. Always be looking for ways to show how much your current clients appreciate your services.

A book that I recommend on the topic of fees is:

- *How to Sell at Prices Higher Than Your Competitors: The Complete Book on How to Make Your Prices Stick* by Lawrence L. Steinmetz

Identify some questions you can ask clients and prospects to assess their needs, wants and value drivers.

EXAMPLE: DEMONSTRATING VALUE

4th Quarter 2011 Financial & Tax Stewardship Meeting Agenda

(Date of meeting)

- Questions
- Open items from prior meeting

Review of Profit & Loss Statement

- Income / Revenue
- Net income
- Go through various expenses (cost of labor, insurance, marketing, etc.)

Review of Balance Sheet

- Cash position
- Line of credit facility

Review of Aging Accounts Receivable

Projection for 2012 & Estimated Tax Payment Trajectory

- Revenues: $
- Expenses: $
- Net Income: $
- Owner draws: $
- Cash in bank Dec. 31, 2011:

1st Quarter Estimated Tax Payment for 2012 Due by April 15

Tax Planning Ideas for 2012

- Putting kids on payroll

Summary and Action Item Review

PACKAGING YOUR SERVICES FOR HIGHER PROFIT

When I first started out in practice fifteen years back, I offered a variety of piecemeal services at standard rates.

For example, I knew several of my clients used QuickBooks and, not knowing any better, I would wait for them to call me to tell me that they had a problem or needed help with something.

In the same way, I had clients that were making decent profits in their businesses and I would wait for them to call my office and schedule a tax planning meeting.

I finally realized that this approach was costing me a ton of money and was not serving my clients well.

When I moved to a more proactive service, I was not only able to serve them better; I was able to charge more.

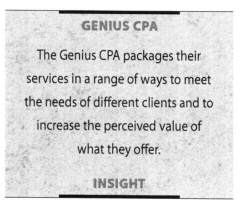

GENIUS CPA

The Genius CPA packages their services in a range of ways to meet the needs of different clients and to increase the perceived value of what they offer.

INSIGHT

The secret to making the move from being a provider of various services to becoming a more proactive business partner was learning how to package my services in the form of a complete solution.

For example, my firm would provide them with a regularly scheduled QuickBooks health check rather than wait for them to call me. Then I incorporated tax planning meetings into the service agreement instead of leaving it up to the client to decide when they wanted one.

The fact is that people are generally happier to buy services as part of a well-structured package than sign up for several individually.

When you can offer your services in packages, it becomes much easier to market yourself to prospective clients. Packages seem to be easier to understand, easier to trust and easier to buy.

It's a lesson to learn from all these fast food places that focus on selling value meals rather than individual items (think of how much money McDonalds has made by offering the cheap plastic Happy Meal toys – the ones your children just *have* to get).

When you package your services, you become seen as an advisor or partner rather than an occasional supplier. The value of the total package can often be seen as much greater than the sum of the parts.

When I made this shift in my services model, it made me different from most of the other accounting firms in my area. I could use that difference to my advantage when marketing for new clients.

One of the keys to getting the best out of having packages is to offer different packages to meet different needs.

People like to have a choice, but it often helps to keep the choice simple, just as a fast food restaurant may offer small, medium and large value meals (sorry, Super-Size has gone the way of the dodo).

Minnesota-based CPA and Superstar member Mike Lewis struggled with pricing when he first started his own practice. He says: "I knew all the services that I could provide, but the question was how to package and price them in a way that eases the sales process?"

He decided to create a range of packages and found it to be a huge success.

"My clients just read the sheet and pick the service packages they want. It is that easy," he comments. They don't question the price because they see the services listed clearly on a description leaflet along with the price for the package.

He continues "It takes all the emotions out of the process. The first client I tried it with signed up for thousands of dollars' worth of services for the first year! I use it to explain my services in a way that clients can easily understand."

That is a common experience among CPAs who opt for the packaging approach that I teach. People can see what they are paying for and make their choices accordingly.

In my practice, the more accessibility the client gets to me and my staff, the higher the fees they pay.

For example, a client who wants to meet with me four a times a year for the Financial and Tax Stewardship meeting will pay more for their services than a client who wants to meet twice.

The following page shows an example of two service packages for small business owners.

 **List all the services your firm provides and then group them into two or three service packages with suitable names.**

EXAMPLE: PACKAGING YOUR SERVICES

GOLD PACKAGE: "Middle of the Line" Small Business Package

PLATINUM PACKAGE: Elite Accounting Package for Small Business Owners Serious About Growing Their Business, Dramatically Increasing Profits and Minimizing Taxes

Service	Gold	Platinum
Quick & Accurate Financial Statements	√	√
QuickBooks Health Checks	√	√
Financial and Tax Stewardship Meetings	√	√
Payroll & Sales Tax Preparation - Monthly, Quarterly & Annual Filings	√	√
Estimated Tax Payments	√	√
"Before the Year is Up" Tax Planning To Maximize Deductions And Minimize Taxes	√	√
Refer-A-Business Cash Rewards Program	√	√
Tax Reminder Service	√	√
Audit Insurance	√	√
Services Rolodex	√	√
"Must Read" BONUS Business Books with Summaries and Value Points		√
Mastermind Group Coaching and Networking Meetings		√

PROMOTING AND CROSS-SELLING A WIDER RANGE OF YOUR SERVICES

Many years ago I learned from the legendary marketer Jay Abraham that there are only three ways to grow your practice:

1. Increase the number of new clients.

2. Increase the fees paid by each client.

3. Increase the frequency of purchase, or sell the same client more services.

One way to get people to buy more services is to sign them up to a package as I just mentioned.

The other is to use cross-selling as the way to get your clients to buy more from you.

This may sound like it calls for a big sales pitch.

But often it's just a matter of telling existing clients about other services you can offer to help them.

Many clients don't know what else you can do for them, so you need to keep them informed.

If you don't currently have a wide range of services, it's a good idea just to ask clients what additional services they need. One way you can do this is by conducting a survey to ask them how you are doing and what else you could do to help them.

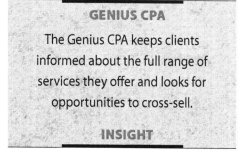

GENIUS CPA

The Genius CPA keeps clients informed about the full range of services they offer and looks for opportunities to cross-sell.

INSIGHT

I have found it very instructive to hear the client's perspective on what we are doing and I have also found it to be one of the best ways to find out about other services we should be offering.

Just as an example, here are some additional services you could be offering:

- Financial planning or wealth management services

- QuickBooks consulting

- Outsourced accounting

- Audit protection

- Business consulting

- Business valuation services

- Payroll services

- Controllership services

- Attest services such compilations, reviews or audits

When you develop additional services, you then need to find ways to let your clients know about them. In the previous chapter, we covered some ways you can do that. For example, you should communicate in your newsletters and during meetings with clients.

If you want to grow your practice, you should never assume that people know what you offer – and never surmise they will not want to engage you for additional services.

 **Make a list of the services you currently provide – and of others you could be providing – then create a plan to communicate them to your clients and prospects.**

Pricing and Packaging:
TOP MISTAKES TO AVOID

Here are common pricing and packaging mistakes that cost CPAs money:

- **Not charging enough.** When your fees are too low, you get into a downward spiral of competing on price that leads clients not to value your services and can force you to reduce the quality of what you deliver.

- **Failing to increase fees.** Many people are afraid to ask clients for increased fees. They often keep fees at similar levels from year to year and even end up providing extra services without charging for them. This becomes an expectation and the longer you go without charging reasonable fees, the harder it becomes to change.

- **Working for hourly rates.** Hourly rates are rarely the best reflection of value for professional services. Take steps to ensure that clients appreciate the value you deliver.

- **Not finding out what clients need.** When you don't know what clients need, it is hard to know the value of what you offer. You will also find it difficult to develop additional services to help them and to increase your profits.

- **Failing to offer packages.** When you combine your services into a package, it helps build a long-term relationship with the client and increase the perceived value of what you do. You move from being a reactive provider of services to a proactive business partner.

- **Not cross-selling.** There are many services you can offer to help meet your clients' needs. It is therefore important to find out from clients what they need and then make sure they know about the full range of services you offer.

KEYS TO SUCCESS

- Too many CPA practices undercharge for their services.

- Competing on price leads to failure.

- The main function of your firm's marketing strategy should be to gain the largest possible share of highly profitable work.

- You must increase the willingness of clients to pay by periodically communicating the value of your services.

- You need to understand what drives value for each of your clients.

- Charging higher fees attracts premium clients and allows you to hire and retain high-caliber staff.

- Failing to charge high fees is usually a reflection of your self-belief (or lack thereof).

- If you believe that your practice delivers superior value, you must charge accordingly.

- You need to position your practice so that you play an integral role in the success of your client's business.

- Packaging your services makes it easier to charge higher fees and be seen as a business partner.

Make a note of the additional key points from this chapter and what actions you are going to take as a result.

8
PARTNERSHIP WITH CLIENTS:

How Your Clients Will Help You Build Your Practice

"Referrals are very powerful. When I refer you, I give a little bit of my reputation away. If you do a good job, my friend that hired you is pleased. But if you do a bad job, that reflects badly on me. People forget that."

IVAN MISNER
FOUNDER, BNI (BUSINESS NETWORKING)

WHEN YOU PROVIDE stellar service to your clients, they will help you build your practice.

You might think that they pay you for what you do and are not obliged to do any more; but, if you build a strong relationship with your clients, you might be surprised at how much they will do to help you. They often see themselves as being business partners and will be happy to support you in whatever way they can.

There are two main ways that clients will help you develop your practice:

- Giving you testimonials

- Providing referrals

These are two very powerful ways to grow your practice and we'll look at each individually.

HOW TO COLLECT AND USE POWERFUL TESTIMONIALS

Without a doubt, one of the most under-utilized, yet most effective, marketing tools for CPA practices is the use of "social proof" in the form of testimonials.

Testimonials are one of my favorite low-cost but high-impact client attraction tools.

WHY TESTIMONIALS ARE SO POWERFUL

In the best-selling book *Influence: The Psychology of Persuasion*, psychology professor Dr. Robert Cialdini explains that the principle of social proof applies when people look to what others have done in a similar situation before they make a decision about what to do themselves.

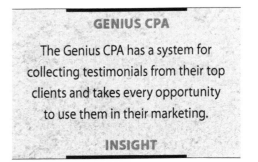

GENIUS CPA

The Genius CPA has a system for collecting testimonials from their top clients and takes every opportunity to use them in their marketing.

INSIGHT

The truth is that, deep down, most of us feel more comfortable when we see someone else using and enjoying a product or service.

There are so many options out there that choosing a product or service can sometimes be a bit scary, so it helps when someone similar to you has taken the risk of checking it out and you feel you can buy with confidence.

Translating this to your practice, testimonials create believability, credibility, and a sense of security for your prospects.

They help to break down the natural barriers and distrust that skeptical prospects may have towards you or your practice at the outset.

You can see the persuasive power of testimonials all around you:

- Flip your favorite book over and read the rave reviews on the back cover.

- Download a movie from iTunes and read the viewer ratings and reviews.

- Purchase a product online and take notice of the testimonials in the margins.

I had a couple of experiences myself just very recently that highlighted the power of testimonials in making important decisions.

The first was when the tires that were on my Beemer seemed to have come to the end of their useful life – probably due to my spirited driving. So, I felt that, before winter came around, it would be wise to get new ones.

Over one weekend, I set aside a couple of hours to do some internet research to see what my options were. I wanted to be sure I was getting the best quality tires available so I wouldn't be back online the following year going through this process again. I came across results of tests performed by companies whose sole function is to test tires. I carefully perused the test results and found them pretty insightful.

Now, here's the interesting (and ironic) thing.

Despite all the tests performed by these specialized companies, I ultimately picked my choice of tires after reading the reviews from other car owners. As you would imagine, I paid special attention to reviews from other Beemer owners because those were the most applicable to me.

Every year, these research companies spend millions of dollars to deploy the latest technology to assess the quality of tires and delve into the most minute of details. Yet, while their analysis carries some weight, a large percentage of consumers like me will evaluate a product or service based on the *experiences* of those who've used it before.

I followed a similar process this past summer when I was looking for a vacation spot for my family. Right after I had created a list of resorts that met our criteria (proximity to the beach, good restaurants, kid-friendly, etc.); I made my final selection based on reading the reviews from past vacationers.

The resort with the larger number of positive reviews won my heart and my business.

It's the same for prospects considering utilizing the services of a CPA firm. They want to know that their personal and confidential information is not being handed over to just anyone. They want to know that you are proficient at what you do, and that others trust you and have had a good experience working with you.

Ultimately, testimonials are a clever tool for lowering the risk that new clients face when engaging your practice.

The more testimonials you have, the greater the chance you have of swaying a skeptic who may be on the fence about trusting your expertise.

Yet surprisingly few CPA practitioners take the time to systematically gather testimonials from their clients.

Well, perhaps it's not too surprising. We don't like to ask our paying clients to go through the extra trouble and we don't feel comfortable fishing for compliments. However, collecting testimonials is simply good business and your clients will usually be happy to oblige.

Florida EA Carl Hanton had been trying to get testimonials from clients for some time and found they would promise to do them but never got around to it. At first, he hesitated to push them on it but then he worked with a few to create testimonials that fairly represented what their problems were and how he helped to resolve them. He then asked them to just write it in an email and send it to him.

He says: "Doing this took just a few minutes with each person, and since it did not involve a lot of time on their part they were happy to do it." He has found the testimonials have helped in his practice. "I think that testimonials are a great arrow in your quiver as long as what is said is true and actually from a client," he adds.

WHAT GENIUS TESTIMONIALS SHOULD SAY

When done well, testimonials can be a strong ally in establishing the credibility of your firm's services.

Here's the catch though…when done wrong, they can actually do more harm than good.

One approach I have found useful in getting great testimonials is a formula I have adopted from Burt Dubin of www.BurtDubin.com. This says that your ideal testimonial should:

- Be a passionate/enthusiastic expression of the benefits and results the client is enjoying/has enjoyed from working with you.

- Begin with a brief statement of the condition before working with you and then a statement of the value received.

- Include the three most significant improvements in their (taxes, profitability, cash flow, number of hours spent, etc.) thanks to those services.

I have used this in a form letter that I send to clients to ask for a testimonial.

The Power of Specificity

An important point to bear in mind is that specifics are compelling. Obtain comments that address a specific benefit or positive result brought about by the use of your services.

These are much more powerful than more generic compliments.

For instance, which of these makes a stronger testimonial?

> "John Doe, CPA is great! I just love him!"

> Or

> "My prior accountant moved out of the state two months before the April 15 deadline, leaving us stranded without a CPA to help us meet our tax filing deadline. On extremely short notice, John Doe, CPA came through for us and he and his staff not only provided us with impeccable tax services, but he also found several errors in our prior year's tax return that led to an additional tax refund of $1,816."

The second testimonial is, of course, the better one. It offers specific, tangible benefits such as:

- He came to my rescue on short notice.

- His firm provided impeccable tax service.

- They spotted errors that led to an additional refund of $1,816.

Here's another example from one of my clients:

> "Your Quarterly Health Check services by your QuickBooks Doctors are excellent because they help me keep my finances on track. The recent catch of a mistake my bank made put $3,107 back in my pocket.

That alone paid off my fees to you. The financial and tax advice you've provided to me as my CPA during the financial stewardship meetings has already proved to be beneficial in saving me money and time."

Damien Romeo, Owner
Retail Maintenance Specialists LLC - Forked River, NJ

Boost Response with Video and Audio

The best thing to do is to get a mix of written, video and audio testimonials. When it comes to video, you can buy a Flipcam now for about $100 and many of your clients are likely to be creating short videos and posting them on YouTube as part of their marketing.

Many will probably quite happily record a short message that you can use as a testimonial. The formula I mentioned works well for videos too.

To get audio testimonials, there are services such as audiogenerator.com and audioacrobat.com that make this easy.

HOW TO USE TESTIMONIALS

You should collect as many testimonials as possible and include them in all your marketing materials. Here are some of the most important ways you can use them:

- **Website.** You should definitely include testimonials on your website. You can sprinkle them in appropriate places – depending on your website design, the margin on the left or right of your home page may work well. However, it's also a good idea to have a separate testimonials page on your website. Prospects will find a long list of favorable comments from your clients to be very impressive.

- **Print ads and sales letters.** Try to include one or two of your best testimonials in your ads and sales letters. You can include more in longer letters. You'll probably find your competitors don't do this, so it helps you stand out.

- **Brochures.** Including testimonials in your services brochure helps get your message across.

- **Business cards.** Use the blank space on the back of your cards for a short testimonial.

- **Ezines.** Including some carefully selected testimonials in your weekly ezine is a great way of supporting your message – it can also act as free advertising for your clients.

- **Newsletter.** You should include testimonials in your printed newsletter – this is also a good place to ask for them.

- **Social media profiles.** Some social media networks, such as LinkedIn, include space where clients can provide a recommendation for you.

- **Testimonial book.** You can even create a special book or sheet to display all your testimonials together. These can be used by potential clients as references. You can give this document a name such as "What People Are Saying About Us."

Testimonials are one of your most powerful marketing tools and you can probably never have too many or use them too often.

HOW TO GET TESTIMONIALS

I know many CPAs find this uncomfortable, but it's perfectly okay to solicit testimonials. You will find clients are usually quite happy to give testimonials as long as you make the process easy.

There are three times that are especially good to ask for testimonials:

- **Client has thanked you for doing a great job.** This is the perfect moment to thank them for their compliment and ask if they would mind supplying a testimonial.

- **You have just completed a task.** You have just delivered a service and you know the client is satisfied. They may not have made any specific comments, so it would be a good chance to ask for feedback, which can then turn into a request for a testimonial.

- **Substitute for a referral.** You have asked the client for a referral and they have not been able to suggest anyone, so ask for a testimonial instead.

I encourage you to incorporate the process of asking for testimonials and feedback into your regular interaction with clients.

You could even do this using a special Feedback/Testimonials form sent out at specific times such as after completing their tax returns. For the best response, be sure to include a self-addressed, postage-paid envelope.

Something to bear in mind is that you should always be willing to provide your clients with testimonials if you can. It's not always possible, but you should aim to support your clients by becoming one of their customers. When you do this, you are in a position to give them a testimonial.

Make Your Testimonials Authentic

I'm sure you've seen websites or sales materials that were loaded with testimonials that all sound as though they were written by the same bad advertising copywriter.

Nothing will ruin your credibility faster than the use of phony testimonials. So make sure they *are* genuine, *sound* genuine, and are *verifiable*.

I know that most CPA practitioners operate with a very high level of ethics, so would probably never consider this, but make sure you never succumb to the temptation to write your own testimonials or to hire someone to write them for you.

All of my client testimonials are set up with each person's name, company name and the town they are located in. They have to look like, and be, real people for believability.

Finally, always get written permission from the client to use their comments in your marketing materials.

 **Identify at least five clients you can ask for testimonials and start using them in your marketing.**

HOW TO GENERATE A STEADY STREAM OF REFERRALS

Even though businesses spend billions of dollars on advertising, the single most effective way of attracting clients is word of mouth referrals.

Yet studies show that only 18% of professional businesses (including CPAs) actively seek referrals from their clients.

Most practices do manage to get occasional referrals but it is usually not part of a planned process. However, the most successful practices are those that ask for and get high quality referrals from their clients.

The good news is that, if you are one of those practices that does not have a program in place for generating referrals, you are sitting on an untapped goldmine of future revenue.

What you need to have in place is a referral system – a methodical process for capturing qualified prospects through your existing clients. By definition, a system is a "process that produces predictable results" and it can be turned on and off at will like a light switch.

WHY REFERRAL MARKETING WORKS

There are a couple of reasons why referral marketing works so well.

People have a natural wish to be helpful and they want to share information about something that has worked out well for them. (However, they will just as quickly talk about things that have turned out badly – such as substandard service.)

Your clients will want to help you because they see themselves as being in partnership with you. Because they interact with your firm, they also see themselves as experts on your practice and what you offer.

So one of the reasons that referral marketing works is that your clients receive something from it as well as giving. They are sharing what has worked for them and they are being helpful. For many, that is a powerful motivator.

Referrals are very attractive to you because clients who are referred to you are your most cost-effective prospects. Once you calculate the lifetime value of a new client, you'll see that you're spending pennies on the dollar to attract referrals from your current client base.

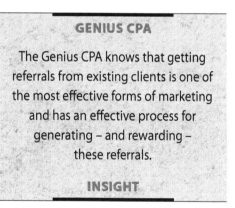

GENIUS CPA

The Genius CPA knows that getting referrals from existing clients is one of the most effective forms of marketing and has an effective process for generating – and rewarding – these referrals.

INSIGHT

In addition, clients who are referred to you will often turn out to be your best clients because they will already have an idea of what you do and the benefits of retaining your services.

Another benefit of getting referred clients is that they tend to be more loyal. If someone has taken a friend's advice through a referral, they are less likely to switch to a new provider as they wouldn't want to embarrass the friend. Referral marketing is therefore the ultimate win-win solution for you and your clients.

They get to be helpful and raise their standing within their network. You get to work with pre-qualified clients who respect your fees and are less likely to jump to a competitor.

Despite this, it's amazing so few practices take advantage of referral marketing.

One CPA who has made powerful use of referrals is Stephen M. Chan from Denver. He strongly believes that relationship plays the most important role between a CPA and their clients and that referral is still the greatest way to get clients.

He says: "I have expanded the referral process and have been aggressively asking my current clients and business professionals for referrals."

He has done this by sending clients a letter letting them know he is able to take on additional clients.

He explains: "I state that if they believe I provide the professional services that they like, I would appreciate if they could recommend people whom they know to me. It is old-fashioned, but it works out very well."

He points out the underlying factor which is that you have to do great work for your clients – otherwise, they would not refer anyone to you.

HOW TO CREATE A REFERRAL CULTURE IN YOUR PRACTICE

There are certain steps you need to take to change the way you think and work in your practice if you want to make referral marketing work.

If you have tried to get referrals without following these principles that may be why you did not get the results you wanted. Here are some of the key principles:

- **To get referrals you must become a referrer yourself.** If you want people to give you referrals, you need to be willing to provide them yourself. The "Law of Reciprocity" says that when you help people, they will feel a desire to help you in return. So make it a habit to give referrals whenever you can.

- **Don't ask for a referral if you won't follow up.** When someone gives you a referral, they are taking a risk with their own reputation. So, make a commitment to follow up on every referral you receive, even if it doesn't seem a good fit. If you fail to follow up, that person will not give you any more referrals.

- **Treat referring clients like royalty.** While every client gets the highest level of service possible, referring clients get treated like royalty in my practice. I know they put their reputation on the line to bring me business. I want them to understand that I value their support.

- **Have a "thank you" culture.** Everyone loves to be appreciated and recognized for their generosity. A sincere "thank you" will open the doors for just about any request.

- **Referrals are everyone's business.** Often, getting referrals is considered to be a sales and marketing activity, but the most successful CPA practices involve everyone in asking for referrals. All the staff have networks of friends and family that need a CPA's services. For best results, incentivize your staff for quality referrals.

When you work on that basis, you are well-positioned for referral marketing success.

FIVE STRATEGIES FOR ATTRACTING REFERRALS

There are many strategies you can follow for attracting referrals. I want to share five of my favorite ones:

1. Immediate Follow-up with New Clients

I've found that the first 24 hours after meeting a new client is a critical time for cementing your relationship and creating a strong impression. This is also the time when your client is most likely going to be telling people about their new accountant. Here are some steps you can take to help them promote you the right way:

- **Email welcome.** Send an immediate "Great to Meet You" email. Be brief and stay focused on how excited you are about helping them.

- **Phone call.** My firm administrator calls the client and has a brief, 10-15 minute chat focused on building rapport and trust with the client.

- **Orientation meeting.** During this meeting, we spend time learning about the client's goals and needs and we also use this meeting to ask for a referral.

- **Handwritten "Wonderful to Meet You" note.** Sending out a handwritten note that gets dropped in the mail immediately after your meeting is a classy and memorable touch. Your client will be impressed by your attention and likely to tell others about it too!

2. Know and Share Who Your Ideal Client Is

I strongly believe that you get what you focus on. If you focus on trouble, trouble inevitably shows up. If you focus on prosperity – you will find that prosperity finds its way to you.

The same is true when it comes to attracting premium clients. It pays to have a specific picture of who you want to do business with. If you don't, then you will get whoever walks through the door (and that could literally be anyone!).

It is especially important to tell your clients what type of prospects you are looking for. You may think that this is being too pushy – but it isn't. If your client wants to help you, they will want to make sure they are sending the right people your way.

If you find it difficult to describe your perfect prospect then you will have trouble attracting referral leads. Your clients won't know who to refer and they will refer contacts that are a bad fit for your practice.

An effective way to do this is to make a list of businesses in your target market that you would like as clients. Then you go through your client list and assess which of your clients would have a relationship with your prospective client.

3. Look for Appreciation Triggers

Always be listening for natural opportunities to ask your client for a referral. The best openings are when your client expresses appreciation for your services. I call these "appreciation triggers." Here are some examples:

"You did a great job – thank you."

"That thought never occurred to me."

"I don't know what I would do without you."

These statements indicate that your client is making a positive judgment about your services. This is the moment where they are most responsive to recommending your practice.

You can follow-up by asking:

> "I appreciate hearing that. You know I was going to give Mr. Erickson at XYZ Company a call, would you mind making an introduction?"

> "Thank you! Could you help me with something? I have been trying to contact Mr. Erickson at XYZ Company for months, what's the trick to getting a hold of him?"

Each of these responses uses a powerful tool – specificity.

Simply asking for a referral often overwhelms the client. However, asking to meet a specific person will often get a "Sure, no problem" answer.

4. Keep Referral Opportunities Top of Mind

Look for subtle, everyday opportunities to ask for referrals. For example:

- Invoices

- Business cards

- Brochures

- Your email signature

- Website footer

- Create an entire referral page on your website

- Social media profiles (e.g. LinkedIn)

Getting referrals is all about keeping the request top of mind with your clients. Let them know that you're always looking for opportunities to help their sphere of contacts.

When you identify places you can ask for referrals, add a statement like this: "We value and reward clients who pass our name along to their friends and family who could benefit from our services."

5. Offer Loyalty Rewards

You can't beat the impact of your client receiving a box of goodies in the mail as appreciation for their loyalty. I call such gifts "Loyalty Rewards."

Imagine their face as they open the box and see a beautiful gift basket with a simple card that says:

> "Thank you for being a great client, partner and friend.
> Here's to another year of working together!"

But, this moment doesn't end there. Your client's co-workers will ask who sent the basket and, when they carry it out to their car, they will be singing your praises. They will tell their spouse about you and their spouse will tell a friend... and so on.

You cannot underestimate the power of rewarding your clients with consistent and heartfelt gifts. They are conversation starters and referral magnets!

According to the Small Business Association, 68% of clients leave their current service provider because they feel unappreciated! No other concern even comes close.

It goes without saying that it's difficult to have a referral program if you have unappreciated clients.

Rewards don't always have to be gifts. They can be anything your client values. Some clients will only feel comfortable with a thank you. Still more would enjoy a token or a gift to show you noticed their effort on your behalf.

I have also had great success using articles, news clippings, and special reports as an "education reward" for my clients. Information is a competitive advantage and most of your clients will not have the time for research. They will be grateful to get the information and will think of you when they use it!

No matter what rewards you set up, you should focus on being consistent in showing your appreciation. Your constant and thoughtful attention will create a cycle of appreciation that clients can reciprocate with referrals.

To create a successful loyalty program you need to develop a loyalty calendar in the same way that we discussed for communication in the chapter on profitable client relationships.

When you work out a schedule on a calendar, you will quickly see that there are dozens of opportunities to touch base with your clients, such as:

- First Year Anniversary

- New Year's

- Valentine's Day

- Thanksgiving

- Labor Day

- The Holidays

- Birthday

Once you have it laid out, you can arrange your gifts ahead of time and have them ready to send on the appropriate days – that way, they get to the client *before* the respective occasion.

Having a calendar also makes it easy to delegate the entire program to a staff member. They simply reference the calendar and send out the appropriate message and gift.

Royalty Rewards

For some clients, you need to go beyond loyalty and offer extra perks. I call these "royalty rewards" because you add a bit extra to the normal loyalty reward for these special clients.

For example, if you send out a gift basket to all your clients on their one year anniversary, consider sending along a gift card as well (with a hand-written note thanking them for the referral).

This technique is powerful because I can almost guarantee that not many are taking the time to connect with their clients this way.

You can enjoy a significant boost in your revenue in the next twelve months by implementing just a few of the techniques in this chapter.

I know because I use them every day to consistently grow my practice. I dominate my area and hold my own against the big boys because my clients love to send me new business. You can put this referral juggernaut to work for you as well.

IT'S NOT ONLY CLIENTS WHO GIVE REFERRALS

While your existing clients may very well be your most important source of referrals, they should not be your only source. In fact, you should seek referrals in as many places as possible.

One important way to obtain referrals is from other business owners and service professionals who already deal with the type of people you want to have as your clients.

So the crucial starting point for attracting referrals from other sources is to identify those folks who might be able to introduce you to your ideal clients. This will vary depending on your market but will usually include professionals such as financial advisers, insurance agents, commercial lenders and attorneys.

The principles of attracting referrals from business owners and service professionals are exactly the same as the ones which apply to getting referrals from clients. For example, after you have identified potential referral sources, you must make it clear to them the specific type of clients you enjoy working with. You would also let them know that you are open to building a cross-referral relationship i.e. you are willing to give referrals as well as receive them.

Make sure you include them in your networking and marketing activity. For instance, you should send copies of your client newsletters to these contacts and attend events and meetings where you will get a chance to expand this network.

When you follow the right strategies and add this group to existing clients as a source of referrals, you'll probably find it is an important driver of your practice growth.

 **Commit now to introducing a referral program in your practice.**

Recommended Resource: CPA Referral Genius System

Although my flagship course *The Genius CPA Marketing System* devotes an entire module to Referral Marketing, CPA practitioners were begging for more. So I decided to take all of my notes, templates, audios, samples and techniques and compiled them into an easy to read, no-holds barred system.

I also went out and interviewed CPA practice owners as well as clients of my accounting practice and asked them what frustrated them the most about CPA referral marketing. Next, I picked the most challenging problems and created strategies that solved them.

Finally, I hired a professional course writer to work with me to make sure that the entire system was crystal clear. The result was the *CPA Referral Genius System: How to Use the Power of Referral Marketing to Supercharge Your Practice's Growth with Less Time and Less Money.*

Here's a brief preview of what it includes:

- Fifty-plus pages of referral marketing techniques with wall-to-wall content, ideas and strategies – no space has been wasted!

- Four audio CDs explaining each of the System modules – you can load each one on to your iPod or MP3 player and listen at your convenience.

- Step-by-step process maps so you can see the entire CPA Referral Genius system and know what to do next.

- A Seven-Day Quick-Start Checklist that you can reference to get you up and running fast.

- Six emails, four referral letters and five postcard templates where you simply plug-in your name and mail!

And that doesn't even touch on all the bonuses. From the first page, you will discover methods of referral marketing that will surprise you with their simplicity and shock you with their results.

For more information, visit:
http://www.TheUltimateCPApractice.com/referrals

Partnership with Clients:
TOP MISTAKES TO AVOID

Here are common mistakes that cause CPAs to miss out on building effective partnerships with clients:

- **Not asking for a referral or testimonial.** Clients enjoy being helpful. They also love to provide information or a helpful tip to their friends. Asking for a referral or testimonial from a satisfied client shows that you recognize their influence.

- **Feeling they will be imposing on people by asking.** You are only imposing if you are pushy and insincere. Following the strategies in this chapter will position you as a professional who values your client's time and relationships.

- **Thinking that clients don't know anyone.** Your clients are far more connected than you think. The notion that most people are connected via six friends or acquaintances has been proven to be true. This is why networks like Facebook and LinkedIn are such huge successes.

- **Being afraid of damaging the relationship with client.** How you approach your clients for referrals and testimonials will determine your success. You will spend most of your time delivering value to your client and you can make asking for testimonials and referrals a natural extension of day-to-day interaction with them.

- **Being afraid they'll say no or reject you.** Sometimes clients won't be able to help you at that moment, especially with a referral. The key is to be consistent in your requests and implement a system to build your relationship over time.

- **Thinking they will give you a testimonial or refer business on their own.** Your clients are busy. At any given moment, they are overwhelmed with priorities and to-do tasks. Even though they may want to refer your practice to others, they may forget or they may not know how. The simpler you make getting referrals and testimonials from your clients, the more success you will have.

KEYS TO SUCCESS

- Testimonials create believability, credibility and a sense of security for your prospects.

- You should collect as many testimonials as possible and include them in all your marketing materials.

- There are three times that are especially good to ask for testimonials:
  1. Client has thanked you for doing a great job.
  2. You have just completed a task.
  3. Substitute for a referral.

- The single most effective way of attracting new clients is word of mouth referrals.

- Clients who are referred to you are your most cost-effective prospects and often turn out to be your best clients.

- Creating the right culture for referrals.
  - To get referrals you must become a referrer yourself.
  - Don't ask for a referral if you won't follow-up.
  - Treat referring clients like royalty.
  - Have a "thank you" culture.
  - Referrals are everyone's business.

- Strategies for attracting referrals.
  - Immediate follow-up with new clients.
  - Know and share who your ideal client is.
  - Look for appreciation triggers.
  - Keep referral opportunities top of mind.
  - Loyalty rewards.

- It's not only clients who give referrals. Expand your reach to other business owners and service professionals.

Make a note of the additional key points from this chapter and what actions you are going to take as a result.

9
PEOPLE AND PROFITS:
Hiring and Motivating Great Employees Who Contribute More to Profits and Success

----

"The way a team plays as a whole determines its success. You may have the greatest bunch of individual stars in the world, but if they don't play together, the club won't be worth a dime."

BABE RUTH
BASEBALL PLAYER, 1895 - 1948

IF YOU WANT to build a successful practice, you need to build one that does not depend on you to do all the work.

That means you need to build a quality team of people you can trust to deliver exceptional services to your clients and that will help you grow your practice.

In this chapter, we'll look at three keys to building a team of superstars. We cover how to:

- Hire the best people.

- Retain and motivate the top performers.

- Ensure they contribute fully to your success.

When you hire the right people and then manage and motivate them, your team becomes part of the reason clients want to work with your practice. They help attract new ones and will enable you to grow.

The quality of your team becomes part of your practice's marketing message and is crucial to your success.

HIRING THE BEST PEOPLE

As your practice grows, you will be spending less of your time working directly with your clients and you need to have staff members that you feel confident are top notch, both in their technical skills and in their customer service.

These days, I often get comments from my clients about how wonderful my employees are. However, I have to confess that it was not always like that.

In my first few years in practice, instead of having an "open door" policy, I had a "revolving door" when it came to employees!

Of course, now as I look back on it, I can joke about it – but it was far from a joke when it was happening.

If I remember correctly, it was seven bookkeepers and two CPAs. And, frankly, I lost track of the administrative assistants who came and went.

It was very frustrating to have such a high turnover because you end up spending a ton of time training people on your systems – time which turns out to be wasted. Then clients hate it because they now have to start the relationship again from ground zero.

However, I learned a lot through those experiences and there are several strategies that I found worked for me when it comes to recruiting and retaining top notch staff.

Here are three of the most important factors I have learned about recruiting high quality staff.

- Design a great recruitment ad.

- Make the hiring process slow.

- Fire fast when things don't work out.

DESIGN A GREAT AD

The first step in the process of hiring good people is designing a recruitment ad that clearly articulates the type of person that will best fit your organization.

You have to describe the character and attitude of the person you are looking for. I believe it is important to hire for attitude and train for skills.

A successful ad will identify exactly the kind of person that you want to have applying for the post. It will also put off the wrong kind of people from applying.

HIRE SLOWLY

It is important to take sufficient time for the process of hiring a new employee. The interview is a vital part of this process and, when I meet with a candidate, I follow a list of questions I've created.

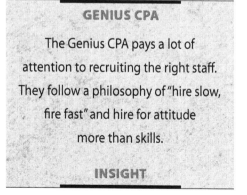

GENIUS CPA

The Genius CPA pays a lot of attention to recruiting the right staff. They follow a philosophy of "hire slow, fire fast" and hire for attitude more than skills.

INSIGHT

This gives me insight into their personality and their way of thinking and helps me decide if they are the right kind of person for my practice.

When talking to other CPAs, I often find they don't prepare adequately for interviews and end up flying by the seats of their pants. Time spent preparing properly for this can save you a lot of trouble later on.

In addition, before you take someone on, it is wise to have a second person interview the candidate. There is no advantage to rushing the hiring process.

You also have to check references by asking probing questions when you contact the person providing the reference and then *listen* to their reply.

Here is one technique that has worked really well for me when it comes to getting unbiased feedback from the reference source.

I will ask all my questions and then, right before hanging up, almost as an afterthought, I will ask, "If there was one thing only, just one piece of advice you were to offer this person (meaning my job candidate) to improve on, what would it be?"

The responses I have received to that one question have led me not to hire several individuals I was almost ready to hire. It has saved me a lot of money.

The reason this question works is because you are first elevating the reference source to that of a mentor, and then you are asking them how the candidate could improve. It usually highlights their biggest weakness.

FIRE FAST

I have been guilty of breaking the "hire slow, fire fast" rule more times than I like to admit, but it's good advice that I came across a number of years back.

It's not a pleasant experience to let someone go, and most business owners, including CPA practitioners, fire slowly because they think, or hope, it will get better.

I read one study that said that the average firing takes somewhere between six and eighteen months after the business owner knew it was a poor hire.

A lot of damage can be done in this time, for example through consistently poor performance and non-compliant work.

In addition to that, the wrong employees can also poison the workplace for other staff members and have a negative affect on clients.

The time you take to get the recruitment process right will be rewarded many times over through your ability to recruit much higher quality staff.

RETAINING AND MOTIVATING THE BEST PERFORMERS

Once you have hired good people, that is only the start of the process. You then need to help them develop to be the best they can be and doing this requires effective leadership.

As part of my monthly "interview an expert" series for my Superstar members, I recently interviewed Michael Useem, Professor of Management and Director of the Center for Leadership and Change Management at the Wharton School of the University of Pennsylvania. He shared a couple of principles with me and my members that I felt were profound.

One of these is the concept which he describes as "honor the room." In the course of contact with people who are your followers or clients, you need to show that you appreciate who they are and what they've done. However, the truth is many people in leadership positions too often fail to take a moment to honor the room.

Another principle he shared that I feel is important in building a strong team is placing the shared interest that you have with other people first against your own personal self-interest.

Michael went on to say that there are lots of phrases used to capture that point, and "servant leadership" is one. In the US Marine Corps, for example, the officers eat last. This implies the officers' personal welfare has to be subordinate to the mission and the safety of the men and women in the unit under their command.

> For more tips from leadership expert Professor Michael Useem, download the interview titled *"Making a Significant Difference in Your Practice and Your Life with Effective Leadership"* as part of the Reader-Only Special Bonus at
> www.TheUltimateCPAPractice.com/free.html

UTILIZE MEETINGS TO SHOW LEADERSHIP AND BUILD TEAMS

One of the most important ways I have found of demonstrating leadership – and building effective teams – is to have weekly meetings to go over work duties and assignments.

I now work only three days per week and on one of the days I come into the office, I allocate half of it for staff meetings and going over high level administrative matters. I meet with my CPA and the manager to make sure the work is being produced to meet my standards.

GENIUS CPA

The Genius CPA knows how to run effective meetings as a way to communicate and improve management without allowing them to waste vast amounts of time.

INSIGHT

In addition to these weekly one-on-one meetings, we have group meetings several times a year.

The purpose and format of these different meetings varies slightly, but I've found that every meeting needs to have the following three ingredients for success:

- **Preparation.** Any information that is required for the meeting should be available to the participants beforehand, such as handouts or action lists.

- **Purpose.** Every meeting of more than fifteen minutes needs to have a purpose that is written clearly on the whiteboard. Everyone understands why they are there and what they are trying to accomplish. Also, having a clearly stated purpose is a gentle reminder to everyone to keep the discussion on point.

- **Discipline.** In your practice, the most valuable asset you have is time. Every minute you spend in meetings represents lost revenue. This means that every meeting should start on-time and end on-time.

The best way to instill this discipline is to demonstrate leadership from the front. Make it a priority to start every meeting on time and follow-through on preparation and restate your purpose.

Here are additional best practices that I find lead to successful meetings:

Create a written agenda. Learning how to create an effective agenda is a great discipline that will help you in all areas of time management. I've found that short agendas are the key to productive meetings. If you have more than three agenda items, consider holding multiple meetings with 10-15 minute breaks in between.

Send the meeting agenda in advance. This gives participants the opportunity to gather their thoughts and bring questions and resources to assist the discussion.

Assign tasks to specific people. Keep careful track of what was decided and who was assigned which task. Most meetings assign vague tasks to "everyone" – which is a recipe for getting nothing accomplished. In my office, shortly after the conclusion of every meeting, an email is sent to the participants with minutes of the discussion and task assignments.

Follow up on action points. Make it a point to follow up on action items in subsequent staff meetings. Your diligence will send the signal that the staff meeting is important and that people will be held accountable for results.

Don't skip regular staff meetings. These meetings should be the heartbeat of your practice. These sessions allow your staff to connect, get informed, and be prepared for their week.

Sporadic staff meetings won't be taken seriously by your team. The rule I use is that "if the office is open, we are having the meeting." Only make exceptions in the rarest of circumstances.

The way many practices work nowadays, some of your staff may not work in your central location. Some may not even be in the same state or country! In this case, a regular staff meeting is even more important. Make every effort to include these off-site team members via a conference line. You can even use a service like www.GotoWebinar.com to share presentation and hand-out material.

In the end, your staff meeting is a foundational discipline that will set the tempo for your practice. Your consistent attention to the effective use of your staff meeting will demonstrate your commitment to excellence, communication, discipline and time management.

Review the process you use for staff meetings to make sure they work effectively. If you never have staff meetings, plan one today!

CELEBRATE VICTORIES – LARGE OR SMALL

I believe that an important part of ensuring that your staff helps you in taking your practice to the next level is to praise and reward them for their contributions.

When someone on my staff goes the extra mile, I will publicly praise them. Sometimes I will send them something to their home like a fruit basket. We celebrate birthdays and we have two parties every year, one after tax season and one during the holidays. You want to have fun.

Running a successful CPA practice takes a team effort to give the client the "ultimate" world-class experience. When it comes to money, if at all possible, give raises when they are deserved, and *before* they are expected.

We conduct annual staff reviews, but if an employee performs at a higher level we don't wait for the annual review. My goal is to compensate my staff more than they would get paid if they were working somewhere else.

 **Look for ways to reward staff for the role they play in your success – especially when their contribution goes beyond what is expected.**

ENSURING STAFF CONTRIBUTE FULLY TO SUCCESS

Another crucial part of encouraging people to give their very best to the success of the practice is making sure that they have a way to share in its performance.

Compensation should be structured so that there is a fixed salary element plus a variable component based on performance and results.

All the jobs in your firm can, and should, be quantified, measured and if you choose, incentivized and rewarded.

I like to see every employee have some opportunity to earn bonus money above base pay, at least based on behavior, but at best, connected to their direct contribution to profits.

In my office, I have three compensation structures for each:

- Seasonal tax professionals

- Accountants

- Administrative staff

> **GENIUS CPA**
>
> The Genius CPA ensures that staff contribute to – and share in – the success of the practice by becoming profit centers rather than cost centers.
>
> **INSIGHT**

As a CPA practitioner, you should look at each job in your firm to see how some, or all of it, can be converted to a profit center.

When I changed my compensation method a few years ago, I immediately saw more than a 30% increase in productivity.

You may wonder how you can translate some jobs into profit centers but it is probably easier than you think. For example, take the job of an administrative person in your office. How can you turn it from a cost center into a profit center?

While the administrative person is on the phone, they could ask a few survey questions to collect information, which helps you segment your client list better. They could also cross-sell other services that you provide. Or, when they are taking calls from prospects, they can capture full and complete information for follow-up, and to build your mailing list.

In other words, they can do more than just answer the phone. Listing out these tasks will enable you to measure the profit-making ones and reward them accordingly.

There's a natural inclination in a professional practice to separate marketing from operations. This leads inevitably to viewing some jobs, and the employees who perform them, as costs rather than as profit centers.

One of the biggest breakthroughs in your CPA practice will happen when *all* employees realize that everything is marketing, and that everyone ought to be involved.

 **Identify how each job in your practice can be turned into a profit center.**

People and Profits:
TOP MISTAKES TO AVOID

Here are common "people" mistakes CPAs make:

- **Trying to do all the work.** You want to start building a high-performing team that you can trust to deliver high-quality services. That will allow you to spend less time producing the work and more time on building the practice.

- **Recruiting too fast.** Too often we recruit employees to fill vacancies without really taking the necessary time to find out if they are the right person. The key point to consider is whether a candidate has the right attitude.

- **Not holding team meetings.** Many practices fail to make time for team meetings or they organize them inconsistently and poorly. A well-planned meeting is an important part of the process of developing people and building a team.

- **Not firing fast.** It's not easy to let someone go if they are not fitting into their role. But hanging on too long to the wrong employees affects the whole practice and causes problems with clients.

- **Not rewarding excellent performance.** It is easy to get into the habit of expecting people to just do their jobs and neglecting to take a moment to encourage them to do even better by recognizing and rewarding exceptional performance.

- **Thinking of employees only as costs.** While employing staff is a major cost for your practice, it is important to think about how the staff member you employ can contribute to the growth of your firm.

KEYS TO SUCCESS

- Strive to build a practice that does not depend on you to do the work

- Build a quality team of employees you can trust to deliver exceptional services.

- Your team can become part of the story that helps attract clients and enable you to grow.

- The first step to hiring quality staff is designing a recruitment ad that clearly articulates the type of person that will best fit your organization.

- When you meet with a candidate, be ready with a list of questions.

- Be prepared to "hire slow and fire fast."

- Before you take someone on, make sure you fully check out the candidate's references and have a second person interview them.

- One of the most important ways to motivate and involve employees is through regular, well-organized one-on-one and team meetings.

- The keys to an effective team meeting are Preparation, Purpose and Discipline.

- Recognize employees for their contribution – especially when it goes beyond what is expected.

- Compensation should have a fixed salary element plus a variable component based on performance and results.

- Aim to turn all roles into profit centers.

Make a note of the additional key points from this chapter and what actions you plan to implement as a result.

10

PERSUASIVE SELLING SKILLS:

Enhancing Your Ability to Get Clients to Say "YES" More Often

----

"Approach each customer with the idea of helping him or her solve a problem or achieve a goal, not of selling a product or service."

BRIAN TRACY
PERSONAL DEVELOPMENT AUTHOR AND SPEAKER

ONE OF THE MOST crucial skills you will need in building your CPA practice is the ability to close a sale.

It's not something we typically learn in college and it's something many professionals feel uncomfortable about.

However, if you want to grow your practice, you will need to persuade more people to sign up for your firm's services.

Many of the processes I've described in this book – establishing your expertise, marketing your services and building relationships – are all about making the sales process easier.

But there comes a point where you have to pin people down and get them to make a commitment.

There are three different situations I'll talk about in this chapter:

- Meeting with new prospects.

- Following up on unconverted leads.

- Contacting previous clients.

In each case, when you follow the right process you will bring a greater number of new steady clients into your practice.

CLOSING SALES WITH NEW PROSPECTS

When all your marketing is in place and you have a steady flow of leads streaming in, you will be at the stage where you are meeting with prospective clients and asking them to sign on the dotted line.

The good news is that closing the sale is actually very simple, when you know how to do it, without feeling pushy and without the prospective client feeling like you're pressuring them.

I've been experimenting with the soft close over the last seven years now on many hundreds of different prospects, and I've made every mistake in the book (and probably a few that aren't in the book), most of which cost me potential clients.

But along the way, I kept getting better and better at it, and started crafting a process that I now consider pretty reliable.

Here's the process I have in place when someone calls my office wanting to meet with me:

1. When the prospect calls, the administrative person in my front office collects all their information on a preliminary interview sheet, including questions about their existing CPA relationship and the reason they want to meet with me.

2. The meeting with me is then scheduled for the following week, usually about five to seven business days after the initial call.

3. In the meantime, we mail a packet of information that they will receive before they come in to meet with me. This contains several items:

   • A sheet on the team members

   • A special report or my book

   • Testimonials

   • Past print newsletters

   It's a thick packet of information, which I call the "Shock and Awe" packet. The goal of this packet is to impress the heck out of the prospect. We also include a "confidential application" in the packet that they must complete.

4. As no one likes to be sold – but everyone likes to buy – I start the meeting with the prospect by asking how they heard about my firm. I ask to take a look at their completed application so I can get a better overview of their revenues, their goals, books they have read, etc.

   I probe into their needs to find out what has been lacking in their existing CPA relationship and learn why they are looking for a change. I also find out about their major challenges and their long and short-term growth plans.

   All the while, I am making notes, and I take a brief look at their business and personal tax returns. I am listening 90% of the time and only interjecting when I want to encourage the prospect to dig deeper into their issues. This is important; most CPAs go astray here, because they are not asking effective questions and they are not attentively listening. Instead, they are droning on about themselves and trying too hard to "sell" the client.

Bernie Marcus, one of the founders of Home Depot, said that whenever a new CEO was hired, they were told, "Don't do anything for the first three months other than shut your mouth, open your ears and go around listening."

That is sound advice that applies not only to new CEOs of organizations, but to practitioners meeting with prospective clients.

By engaging the prospect with good probing questions and active listening, you differentiate yourself from the rest of the practitioners in your area. I then use my notes to recap the list of things they need help on.

5. In the next stage, I talk about what differentiates my firm from the rest; I explain the service packages we offer; and then I go into fees.

Differentiating myself and my firm is important because when I come to the part where I talk about my fees, I don't want the prospect to say that another CPA quoted a lower fee. I have changed the playing field so that the services they will receive from me are perceived to be very different than what my competitors would offer. Remember, if you fail to differentiate yourself from the competition, the only difference the client sees is cost.

6. Next I get the appropriate signatures and payment and my firm has now added a new business client.

7. After the client is signed up, I will briefly meet with my firm administrator to hand off the client paperwork. She takes it from there and will call the client two days later to officially welcome them to our CPA practice. She then schedules their orientation meeting two weeks later.

In the meantime, we will send them a fruit basket and a "Welcome Aboard" card. We are looking at this as a lifetime relationship and a strong referral source, so we invest in it from the get-go!

When you follow this type of process, it becomes more of a business meeting than a sales discussion and the process of signing the client up flows naturally.

I recently saw this working in action when I had a very brief meeting with a new prospective client – the owner of a business generating approximately $800,000 in annual revenue. This experience shows that, following the right system makes client acquisition virtually effortless and almost fun.

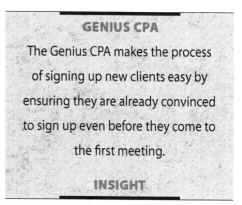

GENIUS CPA

The Genius CPA makes the process of signing up new clients easy by ensuring they are already convinced to sign up even before they come to the first meeting.

INSIGHT

This particular business owner was scheduled to meet with me in my office at 4:00 pm, but she took the wrong exit off the highway and ended up getting to my office at 4:25 pm. I had to be out of my office at 5:00 pm sharp due to another commitment, so I had exactly 35 minutes to understand her needs and convert her from prospect to client.

That may seem an impossible situation but it went perfectly smoothly and resulted in back fees of around $12,000 plus annual fees of some $4,800.

Why was I able to sign her up as a client in such little time? The truth is she was already "warmed" up to me and my firm *before* she even arrived at my office!

She had found me through the internet and was impressed with what she saw and read there. Then, after her initial online contact, she received a package from my office containing more information about my firm. A day before the appointment, she received a call from my office to confirm the date and time.

So, by the time she and I actually met, she already knew she was going to do business with me, as evidenced by the large check she brought with her as retainer for the work my firm would be doing for her.

Think about it... I had only 35 minutes to meet with her and sign her up... a business owner I had never met before.

However, because I had leveraged myself using tools such as my website, an informative (and interesting) package, and high-quality contact from my team, I was able to achieve my goal and sign her up, in spite of the unfortunate delay.

Perhaps someone other than a Genius CPA would think it wasn't possible to sign up someone in the manner I described. They would say that you have to go and visit the prospect at their place of business and that you'd have to meet with them multiple times.

I know this because that is exactly what I was taught when I first went into practice, and that is exactly how I conducted business in the first six or so years. It was painful, demoralizing, and it would suck the life (and energy) out of me.

The system I now follow is not only much more effective, it is much more pleasant and comfortable for everyone.

On the following page, I have given some examples of typical questions you can ask a prospective client when you are getting to know them.

EXAMPLE: QUESTIONS TO ASK A PROSPECT

- Can I first verify your contact information?

- How did you hear about us?

- How long have you been in business?

- What did you do before you started your business?

- What is your current legal structure?

- What tools do you use for record keeping (e.g., accounting software, manual accounting, etc.)

- How many employees do you have?

- How do you process payroll?

- What were your revenues last year and projected for this year?

- What was your net profit last year and projected for this year?

- What is the lifetime value of your typical customer?

- Tell me about your current advisors – accountant, financial advisor and attorney – what do you like about each relationship and what is not working?

- What are your top business goals that you would like to achieve this year?

- What keeps you up at night?

- What are the three big challenges you face as a business owner?

- What is your marketing budget for the year?

- Do you rent or own your business premises?

- Do you foresee the need for financing?

- What differentiates you from your competitors?

- What vision do you have for your business?

FOLLOWING UP ON UNCONVERTED LEADS

In some ways, the easy part of the sales process is converting people who come in for a meeting. The fact they have come in means they are likely to be ready to change and this makes it much easier to help them decide to sign up with you.

A bigger challenge is following up with people who may have been on your prospect list for some time but, for whatever reason, have not yet decided to join you.

I find that most CPAs don't have a good system for following up with the prospects that didn't initially convert to clients.

However, the reality is that most prospects won't sign up with you initially. There are many reasons why the time may not have been right for them to make a change. But, if you have spent the time bringing in leads, you need to make sure you are following up with the ones that don't convert.

There are several reasons why CPAs don't follow up:

- They're afraid of appearing too pushy.

- They're afraid of being turned down or rejected.

- Their negative self-talk gets in the way.

- They're afraid to have to talk about money.

> **GENIUS CPA**
>
> The Genius CPA knows that clients who don't sign up at first contact may have many reasons for that decision. They keep in touch and follow up until the moment is right for that prospect to make a different choice.
>
> **INSIGHT**

However, here's an analogy that I find helpful when thinking about these prospects.

The most easily-accessible fruit on a tree is the heavy, low-hanging fruit.

This is also usually the fruit that is the ripest. You don't have to tug at it to get it off the stem or branch. Low-hanging fruit is the easiest to pick.

It's the same when you think about prospects in terms of how ready they are to work with you:

- Hot prospects are those that are just about to sign up.

- Warm prospects are those who have expressed an interest in working with you, but have not signed up yet.

- Cold prospects are people who have had no contact with you or have already said they are not interested in your services.

Warm prospects are similar to the low-hanging fruit.

If you don't follow up with these people you are missing out on a big opportunity.

I'd encourage you to think back and to go through all your records and compile a list of warm prospects – people who have shown an interest in your services in the past but have not yet signed up.

This list usually ends up a lot bigger than you would expect, especially if you've been in practice for a while but have no tracking system for warm prospects.

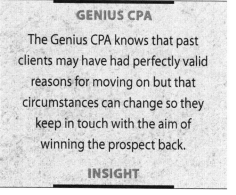

GENIUS CPA

The Genius CPA knows that past clients may have had perfectly valid reasons for moving on but that circumstances can change so they keep in touch with the aim of winning the prospect back.

INSIGHT

When you have the list, it's time to follow up with these people with the objective of setting up a conversation about working together.

You can also use this list to send invitations to your upcoming events, to mail them articles or to send your free weekly ezine.

I have noticed that, in my practice, when I use my "low-hanging fruit" list, I sign on a lot more clients than when I don't use it.

Once I have identified the warm prospects, I call or send an email to the prospect and open it with "I am just checking in…"

The prospect feels comfortable and so do I, because I have to admit that I hate to push myself on others.

This has proven to be a friendly way of seeing where the prospect is in the process. It has helped me convert lots of business prospects into clients, even years after they initially expressed interest in my firm.

 **Go through your records – and memory – and build a "warm" prospect list. Then make a plan for following up with them.**

CONTACTING PREVIOUS CLIENTS

As well as going after your existing prospects, there is another "warm" source of additional revenue for your practice.

This is a source that I have found to be incredibly effective and works without having to run any advertising, ask for referrals or attend any networking meetings.

That source is to reactivate your past clients.

Like every practice, I'm sure you have a number of clients who may have used your firm for one tax season but didn't return the following year.

This could happen for a variety of reasons:

- Moved out of the area.

- Decided to prepare and file their own tax return.

- Switched to a different accountant.

  … Or any one of a thousand other reasons!

No matter the reason, you still have an opportunity to reconnect with these "lost clients" and offer them a way to come "back home."

The best part is that these clients are familiar with your services. There is also every possibility that they had a great experience.

There are plenty of sound reasons why they didn't sign up again at the time – perhaps you just didn't ask them to! They are warm leads that often just need a little extra push.

Here are a few tips on how to approach this group to get them to sign up again.

- **Tax season is your opportunity.** Your lost clients may be looking for a tax preparer. Their situation may have changed. They came to you at one point to solve their problems, so this is the perfect opportunity to get back on their radar screen.

- **Be personal.** Contact these clients in the most personal way that you can. A cold form-letter is not the best option. If you have just a handful of lost clients, then phone them and invite them back to your office. If you have quite a few past clients to contact, then a personalized letter will do the trick.

- **Don't make them feel guilty.** It's okay to nudge your client a bit and let them know you missed them, but don't make them feel guilty for not using your services. Have someone else read your communication to make sure that you don't inadvertently put your client on the defensive.

- **Offer them an excuse to contact you.** The key to bringing back lost clients is to give them a reason to contact you to make an appointment. As I mentioned, tax season provides one opportunity to do this. All you have to do is supply an irresistible offer.

Your offer should be easy to redeem and have an obvious value. It should make your client pause for a moment – offering a refrigerator magnet won't cut it! Your goal is to make the offer stick in your client's mind (and not to their refrigerator) and make it easier for them to contact you rather than ignore you.

 **Create a list of past clients and develop a campaign to target them again.**

Persuasive Selling Skills:
TOP MISTAKES TO AVOID

Here are common selling mistakes that cost CPAs business:

- **Not closing the sale.** We can often end up having pleasant meetings with prospective clients where we let them go away and think about it or just have a general chat. You need to have a process that focuses them to make a decision and sign up right away.

- **Being too pushy.** There are actually two ends of this spectrum. One is that we rush people into making a decision before we have given them time. The other is that we don't press them because we hesitate too much. You need to have a system that leads them to make a decision at the right time.

- **Getting too involved in the details.** The point of a sales meeting is to get the client signed up – not to start going through their issues. It is best to get them signed up and then handed over to the appropriate person in your firm.

- **Not following up with warm prospects.** A big mistake is losing touch with prospects who have expressed interest in your services in the past but did not sign up as the time was not right. You need to have a way of keeping in touch with these people so that you can follow up when the time is right.

- **Not following up with past clients.** It is too easy to assume that past clients left for some negative reason. There are actually many reasons why someone only worked with you for a limited time and you need to go back to them and try and sign them up again.

KEYS TO SUCCESS

- One of the most crucial skills you will need in building your CPA practice is the ability to close a sale.

- The good news is that closing the sale is actually very simple, when you know how to do it, without feeling pushy and without the prospective client feeling like you're pressuring them.

- This is the process I have in place:
  - Administrative person collects information
  - Meeting scheduled after five to seven business days
  - Mail a "Shock and Awe" packet
  - At the meeting, probe their needs gently
  - Talk about what differentiates my firm
  - Get signatures and payment
  - Hand over to firm administrator

- Most CPAs don't have a good system for following up with the prospects that didn't initially convert to clients. However, these are warm prospects that can become clients.

- As well as going after your existing prospects, another warm source of additional revenue is to reactivate your past clients. They are warm leads that may just need a little extra push.

Make a note of the additional key points from this chapter and what actions you are going to take as a result.

MOVING TO THE NEXT LEVEL

I HOPE, as you've read through this book, that you've found motivation, ideas and some inspiration for taking your practice or your career to new levels of success.

The strategies I've shared here were the basis for turning around my practice from struggling to successful.

Over the years, I've seen many Genius CPAs using this information to change the course of not only their practices but their lives.

That may sound dramatic, but I firmly believe that our work is about making life better for our clients, ourselves and our families.

Of course, you're not going to be able to implement everything you read here overnight. It's about following the steps – getting the positioning right, working on your personal brand, promoting your services and creating systems to persuade more and more prospects and clients to develop long-term, profitable relationships with you.

This book gives you the mindset and the strategies you need plus some suggestions of resources you can use to build on that.

However, many CPAs have asked whether there is an option to get more of my involvement and help and to work more closely with me to help them transform their practices and take them to new levels.

So, before we finish, I wanted to tell you quickly about four ways in which you can have my ongoing advice and personal help in building your practice.

GENIUS CPA MARKETING SYSTEM

The Genius CPA Marketing System is your personal tutor for creating a marketing system that will fill your sales pipeline with quality prospects.

It is designed for you to learn and implement at your own pace. And the best part is that it doesn't require that you invest extra money, work more hours, or hire expensive outside help.

Now you can get the perfect collection of marketing strategies and tools that will help take your practice to the next level, including:

- **Four High Quality Audio CDs** that split the entire Genius CPA Marketing System into ten easy-to-understand Genius Modules.

- **Professional Transcripts** of each CD that you can print and use for notes and reference.

- **Genius "Fast Start" Guide** giving quick steps you can take today to begin transforming your CPA practice into a marketing powerhouse.

- **Genius Participants Guide** – 190-page comprehensive binder gives step-by-step assignments, checklists, and tools to keep you on track.

- **The Genius CPA Giant Marketing Toolbox** stuffed with ready-to-use ads, done-for-you templates, checklists, and direct mail swipe files, including:

  o **My Ad Swipe File** – The exact ads that turned my own CPA practice into a market leader virtually overnight.

  o **My Sales Letter Swipe File** – The sales letters I used to hook, inform, convince, and close prospects.

  o **My Testimonial File** – I'll show you my file of business-getting testimonials and how you can easily get your own to boost your marketing.

o **My All Star Interviewing Questions** – List of questions I use to cut through the hype and identify the keepers from the con men.

o **Press Release templates** that you can use to immediately announce your firm's services and generate business starting today.

For more information, visit:
http://www.The UltimateCPApractice.com/genius

CPA REFERRAL GENIUS SYSTEM

Although my flagship course *The Genius CPA Marketing System* devotes an entire module to referral marketing, CPA practitioners were begging for more. So I decided to take all of my notes, templates, audios, samples and techniques and compile them into an easy to read, no-holds barred system.

I also went out and interviewed CPA practice owners as well as clients of my accounting practice and asked them what frustrated them the most about CPA referral marketing. Next, I picked the most challenging problems and created strategies that solved them.

Finally, I hired a professional course writer to work with me to make sure that the entire system was crystal clear. The result was the *CPA Referral Genius System: How to Use the Power of Referral Marketing to Supercharge Your Practice's Growth with Less Time and Less Money.*

Here's a brief preview of what it includes:

• **Fifty-plus pages of referral marketing techniques with wall-to-wall content, ideas and strategies – no space has been wasted!**

• **Four audio CDs explaining each of the System modules – you can load each one on to your iPod or MP3 player and listen at your convenience.**

- Step-by-step process maps so you can see the entire CPA Referral Genius system and know what to do next.

- A Seven-Day Quick-Start Checklist that you can reference to get you up and running fast.

- Six emails, four referral letters, and five postcard templates where you simply plug in your name and then mail!

And that doesn't even touch on all the bonuses. From the first page, you will discover methods of referral marketing that will surprise you with their simplicity and shock you with their results.

For more information, visit:
http://www.TheUltimateCPApractice.com/referrals

SUPERSTAR CPA PROGRAM

In my Superstar CPA Program, I'll let you look over my shoulder and I'll share the detailed marketing action plans that I am working through every month.

So, you won't have to figure out the marketing techniques for yourself. Instead, you just read the plan, listen to the interviews and put the process into motion. I've done all the hard work for you. You need only to see and do.

I can't detail here all of the valuable information that you will get every single month as a Superstar CPA member. You literally will be learning every technique as it rolls-off my testing "assembly line."

That means you'll be the first to market with astoundingly effective marketing tactics that will gobble up clients and leave other CPAs scrambling for crumbs.

Here are some of the goodies I have packed into this program:

- **Featured CPA Superstar Interview.** Listen as I grill our profession's top practice owners and experts. You'll have a front row seat every month as I look for marketing gold.

- **Complete Interview Transcripts.** Unedited word for word printed transcripts to inspire your own marketing techniques and strategies.

- **Private Member Q&A Calls.** Every month, you'll be given free admission to the Superstar CPA Q&A Call where you are free to ask any questions about practice development and marketing.

- **20% VIP Live Event Discount.** Your enrollment in the Superstar CPA program will get you a guaranteed invitation to my special coaching events with 20% discount, where I invite only a small group so that I can give 110% of my attention.

- **Access to the Superstar Member Vault.** Here you will have complete access to my most up-to-date personal library of sales letters, ads, checklists, interview questions, client service agreements and more!

- **Superstar CPA Newsletter.** Every month, I will send you a streamlined Action Guide packed with proven strategies for your practice. I understand you are busy, so only the best tactics will be included. This will quickly become your favorite resource.

This is the type of hands-on, just-in-time marketing advice I wish I had when I first started!

For more information, visit:
http://www.TheUltimateCPApractice.com/superstar

GENIUS CPA PRIVATE COACHING

For those who are interested in a more personal hands-on relationship, I offer a strictly limited number of personal coaching slots.

Running a practice is tough. The margin for error is slim and competition is getting tougher every day. More importantly, you need to reclaim your life and build a practice you can be proud of in the process.

So let me save you years of trial and error. As your coach, I will show you how to:

- **Build An Enduring Brand.** The secret to being recognized as a Genius CPA and not get pigeonholed as a glorified "bookkeeper."

- **Get Out Of Your Own Way.** We'll identify the habits that are sabotaging your success and show you how to break them for good.

- **Lead A Practice Rather Than Being A High-Priced Employee.** I'll show you how to climb back into the captain's chair and create a firm that accomplishes your goals.

- **Transform Your Image.** Learn how to be recognized as a trusted and sought-after business consultant with a financial focus. You can use this new credibility to broaden your practice services, if you choose. (This alone could easily result in a new cash windfall of $20,000-$50,000 per year.)

- **Boost Your Personal Productivity.** Imagine working just three or four days a week and getting more work done! I'll show you the personal productivity secrets that will make you the master of your own calendar.

- **Design Your Own Lifestyle.** Finally you'll be able to live the life you want! Now your practice can empower your lifestyle rather than hinder it.

- **Beat Burnout.** The right coaching will help reignite passion for your practice.

- **Build Predictability And Sustainability Into Your Firm.** We'll explore proven strategies to bust "feast or famine" revenue cycles and turn your practice into a reliable profit generator.

- **Leverage Your Time and Multiply Your Income.** The most critical asset in your practice is your time. I'll show you how to leverage it to multiply your free time and profits.

- **Enjoy Your Clients.** Discover how to design your practice to attract smart and respectful clients who you'll feel comfortable calling friends.

- **Inspire Staff Loyalty.** Your staff is key to scaling your revenue and client base. I'll show you how to turn lukewarm employees into red-hot team members.

- **Broaden Your Horizons.** Take the skills you'll learn and apply them to any business challenge. You'll soon see how your skills are the #1 element for success in any venture!

The Most Comprehensive CPA Coaching Experience Available Anywhere

As your coach, I will focus on providing you with a consistent, high-quality, and productive learning experience. Every moment we spend together will be structured and designed to deliver the maximum value.

Here are the details of what you will get as a Genius CPA Private Coaching Member:

- **Monthly Private One-on-One 45-minute Coaching Calls ($9,000 yearly value).** You and I will speak by phone, one-on-one, every month. During these calls we will discuss your progress and review any questions you may have.

We will start off with a "Practice Jumpstart" where I will work with you to identify the gap between where you are and where you want to be. The Jumpstart phase will include:

o **Setting Smart Goals** as a blueprint for building your practice

o **Complete Practice Audit** to identify areas that need improvement covering your Marketing, Procedures, Culture, Client Service, Service Mix and Delivery.

After the Jumpstart phase, I will help you put what you've discovered into action.

- **Monthly 60-Minute Group Coaching Call** with Recordings ($6,000 yearly value). Once a month, I will conduct a group call with the other coaching members. This will be your own private mastermind for brainstorming, support, and encouragement.

- **Unlimited Email Support ($4,500 yearly value).** Once you join, I will send you my private email address for you to contact me with any questions that can't wait until our monthly call. I will review and respond to your questions within two business days.

- **Monthly Marketing Critiques ($3,600 yearly value).** I'll review up to two marketing pieces per month and send you my critique and recommendations via email.

- **Advanced "Done for You" Services.** Blogging and eNewsletters are the "power" tactics that every practice should deploy immediately. However, you may not have the time to create the editorial content required to get the best return on your investment. As a Genius CPA Private Coaching member, you will get access to my exclusive "Done For You" services. I've packed in all of the pieces you'll need to jumpstart your marketing with relevant content that positions you as an expert.

- **Full Tuition to a Live Seminar ($3,000 value).** You get FREE access to a live seminar I hold where other attendees will pay $3,000 to attend.

Plus much more including *all* the benefits of the SUPERSTAR CPA Program!

Every week, I devote one full day to my coaching members, so it is obvious that I only have a very limited number of places available. For those who want to make major transitions in their practice fast, it may be just what you are looking for.

For more information, visit
http://www.TheUltimateCPApractice.com/coaching

INDEX

Symbols

3Ms of marketing 42

A

Abraham, Jay iv, xv, 175
Accounting Today iv, xii, 68, 90
acquire new clients 13
added value 53
additional offers to clients 132
advertorial 88
agitating the problem 96
anniversaries 153, 196, 197
appreciation triggers 193
article writing 65, 69, 90
asking for referrals 143, 190, 191, 192,
        193, 194, 195, 224
asking for testimonials 183, 186, 187
attentive listening 217
attitude 45
attracting more clients iv, 44, 93, 158
attracting new clients 21, 27, 132, 134
attracting referrals 192, 193
Aweber 146, 154

B

benefits and features 18, 52, 53, 97
billing 160
Bing 117
birthday cards 145, 153
blocking time on calendar 25, 26
blog creation 111
blog, generating interest 112
blogging 106, 111, 112, 113
blogging benefits 111, 112
blogging popularity 111
blog hosting and software 112
blog purpose 112
boring marketing 100, 137, 142
building additional revenue 132
building a strong team 205

business books 36, 37, 75, 126, 169
business cards 85, 93
buying advertising 42

C

call to action 99
canned newsletters 137
canned websites 107
card decks 90
changing your fee structure 132
charity 93
checklists 21, 22, 230, 233
classified advertising 88
clear message 42, 43, 50, 86
client appointments 25
client communication 137
client-generating activities 27
client newsletters 137, 138, 140, 141,
        142, 143, 146
client newsletter service 144
client newsletters, ROI 139, 140
client newsletters, top 10 tips 141
client newsletters, using own voice
        141
client retention 134, 135, 138
client touch plan 153
client touch points 146
closing the sale 216
collecting testimonials 182, 183, 185
Collins, Jim 36, 148
commoditization 15, 41, 158, 160
Commoditization Litmus Test 15
commodity 15, 16, 42, 158, 166, 167
commodity thinking 158
communicating value 168
communicating your positioning 42
competing on price 52
competitive advantage 9, 151, 196
confidence 98
Constant Contact 146
contact information, collecting 86, 88,
        90, 108, 110, 122

converting prospects 138, 146, 219, 222, 230
copywriters 96
cost of referrals 189
CPA Referral Genius System iv, 198, 231
creating systems 21, 229
creativity 34, 35, 101, 160
credibility 68, 111, 183, 234
cross-selling 132, 136, 138, 143, 175, 210
customer relationship management (CRM) 146, 150, 151
customer service 33, 34, 36, 202
customized newsletters 138

D

databases 150, 151
deepening relationships 137
defining your target market 43, 49
delegation 20, 27, 28, 126, 196
demographics 44, 46
differentiating factors 53
differentiation 14, 15, 42, 83, 141, 167, 218
Digg 125
direct mail 86, 89, 100, 230
direct response 84, 90, 101, 107
display advertising 88
documented systems 20, 23
Do Not Call rules 93
drivers of lifetime value (LTV) 158

E

education-based marketing 62, 65
effective systems 13
effective working procedures 22
efficient working 13
Elance.com 67
email addresses 108, 110, 236
email list 67, 78, 110, 127, 148

email newsletter (ezine) 146
email signature 151, 194
email systems 147
employee compensation 210
employee performance sharing 209
employee praise and reward 209
employee raises 209
employee recruitment process 21, 203
employee references 204
E-Myth xiv
entertaining 34, 138
entrepreneur iv, 2, 36
establishing your credentials 96
existing clients 46, 132, 135, 143, 175
expanding range of services 132
expert positioning 46, 49, 62, 63, 64, 65, 68, 69, 75, 76, 78, 92, 96, 136, 158, 206, 215, 236
extraordinary 33, 34, 35, 36
ezines 146, 147, 153, 186
ezines, tips for creating 147

F

Facebook 111, 113, 124, 126
feedback 54, 187
field of expertise 64
firing employees 205
five Cs of value 162
flash animation 109
Flickr 124
following up referrals 191
following up with old prospects 222
freelance writers 67
frequency of purchase 175

G

Genius CPA Marketing System iv, 197, 230, 231
Genius marketing 83, 84, 86, 87, 88, 94
Gerber, Michael iv, xiv, 36

getting referrals 194
gifts 33, 35, 36, 153, 195, 196, 197
giving referrals 191
Google 115, 117
Google Analytics 127
Google Maps 117
Google Places 117
Google Plus 124
go-to expert xi
guarantees 33, 92, 98, 197

H

Halbert, Gary iv, xv
Hansen, Mark Victor iv
headlines 92, 96, 101, 109, 111, 112, 147
Herr, Jim 17
higher fees 44, 168
hire slow, fire fast 204
hiring quality staff 202, 205
Hogan, Kevin 148
home page 108, 185
honor the room 205
HootSuite 126
hourly rates 26

I

ideal clients 42, 43, 44, 45, 46, 48, 63
ideal market 43, 47, 52, 55
ideal prospects 42
ideal target market 50
identifying your market 43
in demand status 168
ineffective websites 108
Infusionsoft 146, 150, 154
internet 77, 105, 181, 219
interviewing new employees 203
iTunes 75, 181

K

keeping in touch with clients 132, 146
Kennedy, Dan iv, xv, 157
keywords 113, 115, 118, 127
knowing value of client 133

L

Law of Friends 148
leadership 205, 206
lead generation 21, 76, 77, 87, 216
leverage 78, 235
lifetime value (LTV) 133, 134, 137, 158, 189
LinkedIn 113, 124, 126, 186, 194
litmus test 15, 17, 41
local directories 116
local search 88, 117
long-term clients 106
long-term goals 25
low-paying clients 45
loyalty calendar 196
loyalty program 196
loyalty rewards 195
lumpy mail 100

M

mailing lists 47, 55, 89, 143, 211
managing email lists 146
market gaps 47
marketing materials 15, 43, 100, 185
marketing message 50, 51, 53, 54, 202
marketing-minded 13
marketing process 43, 49, 125
marketing strategy 42, 55, 162, 230
maximizing lifetime value (LTV) 13, 160
measuring effectiveness 83, 118
measuring results 89, 102, 126
media coverage 68
meeting agendas 168, 207

meeting prospects 15
mental shift 13
mindset xii, xvii, 1, 2, 3, 158, 229
motivating staff 201, 202

N

name awareness 83
networking 55, 72, 73, 75, 93, 174,
    224
networking skills 72, 73, 74, 75
new clients 85, 131, 135, 136, 137,
    145, 172, 175, 182
newsletters 137, 138, 140, 141
non-tax season 21

O

offering additional services 175
office redesign 101
office systems 21
old-style networking xix, 45
online advertising 117
online marketing xix, 75, 77, 87, 88,
    105, 126
opportunity cost 27
opt-in box 110
outsourcing 126

P

packaging services 100, 132, 136, 171,
    172, 173, 175, 218, 219, 220
pay-per-click (PPC) 117, 118
personal brand 61, 62, 63, 64, 66, 67,
    69, 72, 75, 76, 77, 78, 85, 105,
    229
personality 49, 75, 107, 203
podcasting 63, 75, 76
poor marketing 83, 86
positioning 50, 61, 64, 229
positioning your practice 42
postcards 89, 100, 153, 154, 198, 232
post-headlines 96

practice owner 13, 22, 107
practice story 17
pre-headlines 96
premium clients 193
premium fees xvi, 16, 42, 166, 167
premium service 166
presentations 67, 68, 76, 78, 208
press release content 92
press release distribution 92
press release process 90
press releases 69, 78, 90, 91, 92
press release topics 91
pricing 42, 158, 172
pricing based on value 160
proactive business partner 171
proactive service 168, 171
procedures, documentation 20, 21
procedures manual 19
process implementation 22
profitability of your practice 157
profit margins 15, 158
promoting your practice 75, 87
promotion 55, 64
prospects 51, 54, 62, 87, 90, 107, 133
prospects calling you xv
prospects, hot 223
prospects, warm 223, 224
PRWeb.com 92
P.S. at end of letter 99
psychographics 44, 45, 46, 48
publicity 69, 86, 90
public speaking 27, 28, 65, 67, 68, 75,
    76

Q

questions for prospective clients 220
QuickBooks 5, 171, 174, 176, 184

R

reactivating past clients 224
reasons business owners change CPA
    136
recognized expert 61, 62, 63, 67, 68,
    75, 90, 91, 124, 142
recruit and retain high-caliber staff
    203, 205
recruitment advertising 203
referral letters 198, 232
referral magnets 195
referral marketing 189, 190, 191, 197,
    198, 231, 232
referral process 190
referrals 48, 55, 138, 190, 191, 195,
    219
referrals from other professionals 85
referrals, key principles 3, 191
referral slips 36
referrals, use of 190
referring clients 191
reinforcing value 167
reinvention 6
relationship building 86, 87, 107, 108,
    123, 125, 132, 135, 136, 150,
    215
relaxation 24
reputation 90, 99, 123, 124, 142, 191
retaining existing clients 13, 134
review sites 116, 117
right-sizing fees 159

S

sales letter 98, 99, 100, 230, 233
sales pipeline 230
sales process 172, 215, 222
scarcity 99, 168
scheduling appointments 26
screening calls 25
search engine optimization (SEO) 115
search engine ranking 111, 115

search engines 115, 117
segmenting your market 47, 63, 210
self-help 1
seminars and workshops 76
sending clients referrals 33
setting fee expectations 168
shift your energy 13
signing up new clients 220
small businesses 2, 62, 63, 64, 91
small business expert 62, 64
small things matter 36, 149
social media xix, 77, 79, 106, 111, 113,
    123, 124, 125, 126, 186, 194
social networking 77, 125
social proof 97
special reports 66, 67, 78, 88, 196, 217
sponsorship 93
staff annual reviews 209
staff group meetings 206
staff meetings 26, 206, 208
staff one-on-one meetings 206
staff recruitment and retention 47, 202
standards 12, 22, 206
Straight Talk About Small Business
    Success In New Jersey iv
strategic objective 9
strategic work 13, 14, 20, 23, 28
StumbleUpon 125
sub-headlines 111
success conditioning 36

T

taking action 62, 96, 99, 127, 131
target market 18, 46, 50, 55, 57, 63,
    66, 89, 90, 193
target market problems 3, 42, 50, 64,
    66, 160, 165, 182
tax season xvi, 10, 20, 21, 24, 35, 76,
    159, 209, 224, 226
tearsheets 90
technical knowledge xi, 12
technical skills 202

teleseminars 77, 79
testimonials 98, 109, 117, 142, 167,
      181, 183, 184, 185, 186, 217,
      230
testimonials, benefits 181, 182, 183
testimonials, using 185, 186
testimonials, video and audio 185
thanking for referrals 196, 197
three ways to grow your practice 175
time management 24, 208
time spent on marketing 14
to-do lists 25
total client value 13
trade shows 93
training staff 202
turning jobs into profit centers 210
TV and radio advertising 89
TweetDeck 126
Twitter 111, 113, 124, 126
two-step marketing 86, 89
two-way communication 112, 124

U

undercharging 157, 161, 166
Unique Service Proposition (USP) 10

V

Valpaks 90
Vaynerchuck, Gary 63
video marketing 75, 76, 124, 137, 185
vision 9, 22
voice and fax broadcasts 93

W

Wal-Mart pricing 166
webinars 77
web pages 109, 115
website analysis 127
website design 110, 185
website evaluation 107
website key pages 108

website navigation 111
website referral page 194
website traffic 75, 106, 111, 112, 113,
      114, 115, 117
website visitors 106, 109
weekly staff meetings 206
white papers 66, 91, 108
word-of-mouth marketing 55
WordPress 112
working on your practice 13
world class 33, 209

Y

Yahoo 117
Yellow Pages 85, 88
YouTube 75, 79, 124, 185

Reader-Only Special Bonus ($328 Value)

4 FREE Gifts To Help You Build Your Own Ultimate CPA Practice

($328 Value)

As a special thank you for buying this book and to help you take even faster steps to creating the Ultimate Practice, I have created a special bonus package worth $328 that you can download right away.

Here is what you'll receive inside the Ultimate CPA Practice Acceleration Kit:

Special Report:

7 Golden Nuggets for The Ultimate CPA Practice

Interviews in downloadable mp3 audio format:

Interview with publicity expert Joan Stewart, titled *How to Promote Your CPA Practice Using Online and Offline Publicity Tools and Strategies.*

Interview with pricing expert Jason Marrs, titled *Common Mistakes Practitioners Make With the Fees They Charge and How to Avoid Them!*

Interview with Michael Useem, leadership expert and professor at the Wharton School of the University of Pennsylvania, titled *Making a Significant Difference in Your Practice and Your Life with Effective Leadership.*

To get instant access to your pack, go here:

www.TheUltimateCPAPractice.com/free.html